A Year with
Saint Thérèse of Lisieux

SHIRT *of* FLAME

A Year with
Saint Thérèse of Lisieux

SHIRT *of* FLAME

HEATHER KING

PARACLETE PRESS
BREWSTER, MASSACHUSETTS

Shirt of Flame: A Year with St. Thérèse of Lisieux

2011 First Printing

ISBN 978-1-55725-808-3

Library of Congress Cataloging-in-Publication Data

King, Heather, 1952–
  Shirt of flame : a year with St. Thérèse of Lisieux / Heather King.
    p. cm.
  Includes bibliographical references (p.   ).
  ISBN 978-1-55725-808-3 (paper back)
1. Thérèse, de Lisieux, Saint, 1873-1897. I. Title.
  BX4700.T5K56 2011
  282.092—dc23

2011022594

10 9 8 7 6 5 4 3 2 1

Published by Paraclete Press
Brewster, Massachusetts
www.paracletepress.com
Printed in the United States of America.

For Alfred Leroy Davis III

The dove descending breaks the air
With flame of incandescent terror
Of which the tongues declare
The one discharge from sin and error.
The only hope, or else despair
      Lies in the choice of pyre or pyre—
      To be redeemed from fire by fire.

Who then devised the torment? Love.
Love is the unfamiliar Name
Behind the hands that wove
The intolerable shirt of flame
Which human power cannot remove.
      We only live, only suspire
      Consumed by either fire or fire.

—T.S. ELIOT, from "Four Quartets"

CONTENTS

INTRODUCTION   xi

JANUARY   EARLY LOSS   3
(On Facing Ancient Grievances)

FEBRUARY   THE CONFLUENCE OF WILL   13
AND GRACE
(On Illness and Healing)

MARCH   THÉRÈSE'S SECOND   25
CONVERSION
(On Learning to Serve)

APRIL   THE PAPAL VISIT   35
(On Daring to Ask)

MAY   POVERTY, CHASTITY,   47
OBEDIENCE
(On Radical Social Conscience)

JUNE   THE CONVENT   57
(On Shedding Our Illusions)

JULY   THE LITTLE WAY   69
(On the Martyrdom of Everyday Life)

AUGUST   ARIDITY   81
(On Praying Without Ceasing)

SEPTEMBER   THE LONG, SLOW DECLINE   93
OF THÉRÈSE'S FATHER
(On Being Stripped Down)

OCTOBER THE STORY OF A SOUL   105
         (On Offering Up Our Work)

NOVEMBER MY VOCATION IS LOVE!   115
          (On Letting Our Flame Burn Hot)

DECEMBER THE DIVINE ELEVATOR   129
          (On Facing Death with Joy)

APPENDIX A: THE MARTIN FAMILY, IN BRIEF   139

APPENDIX B: CHRONOLOGY OF THÉRÈSE'S LIFE   141

NOTES AND PERMISSIONS   145

SELECTED BIBLIOGRAPHY   157

INTRODUCTION

ST. THÉRÈSE OF LISIEUX lived only twenty-four years, from 1873 to 1897. She was the youngest of five daughters, all of whom eventually became nuns. When Thérèse was four, her mother died. From the age of nine she had a vocation. When the Carmelite convent where she longed to make her home said they couldn't take her until the standard age of twenty-one, she badgered her father to take her to Rome so that she could appeal, in person, to the Pope. In 1888, at the age of fifteen, she entered the cloister. Her life in the convent was unremarkable. She did not distinguish herself spiritually or in any other way with her fellow nuns. But inside her soul, a conflagration raged. Inside she was on fire with love.

Inside, she consented to wear the "intolerable shirt of flame" (see the passage from T.S. Eliot's poem on page vii) that can either purify or destroy, redeem or eternally torment. Inside, she allowed her heart to be consumed—invisibly, in obscurity—by the cleansing blaze of Christ's love. So vivid was the phrase from Eliot's poem, so beautifully did the image evince Thérèse's inner life, struggles, and spiritual evolution, that I chose *Shirt of Flame* as the title of this book.

In fact, Thérèse must have exhibited some small outward spark. For in the winter of 1894, under orders from her second-oldest sister Pauline (Mother Agnes of Jesus, at that time prioress of the convent), who in turn had been urged by Sister Marie of the Sacred Heart (Thérèse's eldest sister Marie), Thérèse began writing a memoir of her childhood, the development of her life in Christ, and her six years of religious life. The result, "Manuscript A," comprises chapters 1 through 8 of most editions of her autobiography, *L'histoire d'une Âme* (*The Story of a Soul*).

She completed the rest of the book in stages. A letter written to Sister Marie of the Sacred Heart while on retreat in September 1896 became "Manuscript B," comprising chapter 9 and containing the well-known treatise "My Vocation is Love." Meanwhile, Thérèse had begun coughing up blood, a harbinger of what would become a two-year, increasingly excruciating onslaught of tuberculosis. In June 1897, only three months before Thérèse's death, Mother Marie de Gonzague, the superior of Carmel at that time, directed her to write what would become "Manuscript C," comprising chapters 10 and 11 of *The Story of a Soul* and including, among other things, the "Divine Elevator" passage and an explication of Thérèse's "little way." Full of charity and good cheer to the end, she died in agony, with no pain medication, on September 30, 1897, crying: "I love You!"

The Story of a Soul, published posthumously and heavily edited by Pauline, became an immediate bestseller. The entire world seemed to respond to the simple, childlike nun who was nicknamed "The Little Flower." In an unusual move, Pope Benedict XV waived the usual fifty-year beatification requirement. Though others had waited centuries to become saints, Thérèse was canonized a mere twenty-eight years after her death.

At first glance, her observations can seem commonplace: "At each new opportunity to do battle, when my enemies come and provoke me, I conduct myself bravely" [*SS*, p. 238]. "God wouldn't know how to inspire desires that can't be realized" [*SS*, p. 230]. "Now I no longer have any desire, unless it's to *love* Jesus passionately" [*SS*, p. 201].

This deceptively simple book, and the inner journey it describes, however, continue to instruct, confound, and inspire. As writers from Father Ronald Rolheiser to Dorothy Day have noted, Thérèse was a mass of contradictions: pampered child, yet with a will of iron; possessed of a lifelong, innate, and in the end conscripted loneliness, yet able to embrace the whole world; essentially unschooled, yet one of only three women (along with St. Teresa of Avila and St. Catherine of Siena) made by papal decree a Doctor of the Church; a spiritual giant whose philosophy has come to be known as "the little way."

I think we all heave a sigh of relief when we hear "the little way." When we try to practice it, though, we tend to find that the way is not so little, or rather not so easy. We see that "the little way" is grounded in great paradox, great complexity, and great labor. Thérèse tells in *The Story of a Soul*, for example, of the nun who sat behind her in choir who made a supremely annoying noise, like "two shells rubbing together." Thérèse trained herself, literally breaking into a sweat from the effort, to refrain from turning around and giving the woman a nasty glare. Try that next time someone jumps the line at the bank, or cuts you off as you try to merge onto the freeway, or insinuates that you're not working hard enough! Begin to ponder the years of discipline, prayer, and the turning of the will toward God required for such a "tiny" taming of the instincts.

Maybe Thérèse's point is not that little sacrifices are easy, but that little sacrifices—opportunities that present themselves hundreds of times daily—are pleasing to God. Big things, too—though what is a big thing, really? You broker peace in a war, but you can only broker peace if you're at peace with yourself. You free the enslaved, but to free the enslaved you have to have done the long, hard, lonely work of being freed from your own inner bondage. All things, big and small, are a version of this: you allow your ego to be crucified.

To allow your ego to be crucified, you have to get very close to Christ. You have to believe with all your heart that Christ is a friend. Thérèse's gift was to have penetrated the Gospels in such a way that she discovered a way of being with Christ that we'd never quite seen before. She wanted to marry him, to be consumed by the fire of his love, to die for him. Like most of us, however, she knew herself to be too small, too little, too unworthy, too unremarkable, too bereft of talent and glitter for so great a task. So she opened a whole new door by daring to believe that Christ would meet us where we are and lift us up to him.

She offered to be his plaything—his rubber ball that he kicked into a corner when he got tired, that he *pierced,* if he chose. She prayed for him, breathed for him, slept for him, ate for him: "I imagine myself at Nazareth, in the house of the Holy Family. If, for instance, I am served with salad, cold fish, wine, or milk with rum [in the infirmary], I offer it to St. Joseph, and think: *Oh, how good that will be for him!* To our Blessed Lady I offer hot foods and ripe fruit, and to the Infant Jesus our feast-day fare, especially broth, rice, and preserves. Lastly, when I do not like the food at all, I say cheerfully: 'Today, my Little One, it is all for you.'"

Much as we long for such closeness, most of us are also afraid: that we're not good enough, not clever enough, not deserving enough. But maybe the real reason is that we've been frightened by the wounds of childhood into closing our hearts. We're afraid of getting hurt again. As a child, when presented with a sewing basket of ribbons and trimmings by her sister Léonie and invited to choose, Thérèse famously replied, "I choose all!"

I don't know about you, but I'm more the type whose response would have been: "I choose none." If you ask for "all," people might think you're selfish. If you ask for all, you might not get anything. If you keep your wants to a minimum, you don't have to risk rejection or disappointment. If you choose nothing, you never have to suffer the pain of deterioration and loss. As the oldest of six children in a family affected by alcoholism, the delusion that if only I were good enough, accomplished enough, pretty enough, perfect enough I could save them ("them" being my family, the poor, the sick and suffering, the world) had been seemingly hard-wired into my psyche since practically my first sentient day. I'd come a long way, but from a very young age, my "strategy" for getting through the world had been to hoard and to slave. We have to want it all. We have to have the courage to open our hearts and want all that God has to give us, knowing that we may be disappointed.

Thérèse wanted "all," but to her that meant she wanted all the suffering. The scandal of Christ is that to have a relationship with him means to share in his suffering. The truth is that we *are* going to share in his suffering, whether or not we want to, whether or not we know it as such. Christ invites us to share in his suffering consciously. He invites us to share in his suffering, not by taking on extra suffering but by joyfully participating in the mostly small but myriad instances of suffering that come to us unbidden each day. He invites us to share in his suffering and to thereby break through to new life, new wholeness, a new level of awareness.

Thérèse devoted her short but almost unimaginably intense life to coming awake in this way—a task she accomplished not by doing great things, but by doing the smallest things with utter attention and utter love, and by recognizing the glory in the smallness of others. "To pick up a pin for love can convert a soul." "Everyone you meet is fighting a hard battle." "Nothing is sweeter than to think well of others." Nothing is sweeter and just about nothing is harder. We want to think well of ourselves, not of others. We want to judge so we'll look better in comparison. (Here's a simple test, offered by a priest friend, for gauging your spiritual condition: see how you react when another person is praised in your presence.)

I, too, wanted to come more awake in Christ. I, too, wanted to abandon myself: body, mind, spirit, soul. I didn't want to be emotionally or materially stingy. I didn't want to live in crabbed fear. I wanted to be like St. Thérèse of Lisieux saying, "I choose all!" "I'm of a nature such that fear causes me to draw back," Thérèse noted; but "with love, not only do I go forward, but I fly. . . ." Me, too: but how to *get* to the love?

I wasn't sure, but I did know that St. Thérèse was just as alive today as she had been in the late 1800s, and every bit as relevant. She didn't speak directly to "romance and finance"—those two areas of perennial human struggle—but almost everything she did say bore on the subjects. From her spare, cold cell, she studied the human heart. From behind the grille, she looked out at the whole of the human condition. Within the walls of her cloistered convent, she made the perilous journey toward becoming a fully realized human being.

Why "walk" with a saint at all? What does it matter if a person is a saint? In one way, it doesn't; in fact, one of my abiding obsessions is the "unsung saint": the person who, unlike Thérèse, is *never* noticed. But here's why saints are interesting: Saints are exceptional. Saints are extreme. As William James observed in *The Varieties of Religious Experience*: "There can be no doubt that as a matter of fact a religious life, exclusively pursued, does tend to make the person exceptional and eccentric . . . It would profit us little to study [a conventional, ordinary] second-hand religious life. We must make search rather for . . . individuals for whom religion exists not as a dull habit, but as an acute fever rather."

I, too, wanted to experience religion as an acute fever:
to some extent, in fact, I already did. My heart had always
burned with holy longing. I had always ached for someone
or something upon whom to lavish my love. That I had come
to God, then to Christ, through alcoholism was no accident,
for in spiritual terms my craving for drink had been a thirst for
the infinite, gone badly awry. That the obsession to drink had
been removed one long-ago month at a Minnesota rehab was
the central fact of my existence. That after being lost for so long
I'd found my way as well to writing and the Church was the
miracle around which constellated, on my better days, boundless
gratitude, astonishment, and joy. I'd been sober for twenty-two
years, a writer (after giving up my hateful job as a lawyer) for
fifteen, a Catholic for thirteen. I saw my writing as vocation, my
conversion as a kind of marriage, and sobriety as the deepest
available way to do unto "the least of these" (and myself).

My outer life was active but not crowded. I cooked dinner
for friends, took road trips, drove to jails, psych wards, and
rehabs to share my experience with other drunks, reveled in
a love-hate relationship with my adopted city of Los Angeles.
But my real life was an inner journey, lived at fever pitch. I
prayed, I wrote, I went to Mass and Confession, I took long,
solitary walks, I made retreats at convents and monasteries.
I thought about God incessantly, I loved Christ, I saw the
Church as my Mother, I had labored to carve out a religious
path in the midst of a resolutely secular culture.

Like every human being, I had also known intense,
prolonged suffering. Over the course of the fifteen years

I'd been writing, I had published dozens of essays and two memoirs: one about addiction as spiritual thirst; the other the story of my (ongoing) conversion. I had been anthologized, given more interviews than I could count, written and recorded over thirty stories for National Public Radio's "All Things Considered," a show to which twelve million people listened—and yet my career seemed to have not *quite* caught fire. My literary agent kept saying, "Your breakthrough will come," and though I was abjectly grateful ever to have been published at all, the breakthrough, or the breakthrough I'd envisioned, had not come.

In the last decade, I had also undergone a series of deeply painful losses. A sixteen-year marriage had ended in divorce and annulment. I'd had a brief (brief because I'd gone against medical advice and refused radiation and chemo) bout with cancer. I'd watched my beloved father die a slow, painful death. My siblings and I had moved my mother, who suffers from Alzheimer's, into an assisted-living facility. And then, just as I'd turned fifty, I'd fallen in love—incandescently, excruciatingly, in love—with someone who didn't, couldn't, wouldn't love me back.

I was not in despair, but I did not understand where my love was "supposed" to go; upon whom or what this explosive, burning desire of my heart was supposed to focus. No matter which way I turned, I found a blank wall. I felt baffled, frustrated, even ashamed, I felt as if, over and over again, I'd given birth to a stillborn. Did passion, discipline, and hard work count for nothing? Making my way alone was hard enough; did I also, after years of pain, still have to feel conflicted and semi-obsessed about the unrequited love?

Not to put too fine a point on it, but to be a woman—aging, single, and without significant means—is a fairly deep kind of poverty. I didn't mind not having a lot of money. I didn't mind—and this is not in any way to diminish my many generous, kind, loyal friends—having no particular support, validation, encouragement, or companionship. I didn't mind that for over twenty years I'd been writing moral inventories, examining my conscience, working with a spiritual director. What I did mind was the sense that my life was *to bear no fruit at all*.

No matter which direction I looked, I saw more suffering, and the only reason I knew I was marginally on the right path was that for the most part I did not inflict my suffering on others. I went out to the world with a basic sense of gratitude, wonder, joy; and the joy was not faked. I had not lost my sense of compassion; if anything, my compassion had deepened. I had not lost my sense of humor. But I was also in a kind of dark night of the soul that I couldn't see my way out of. The only thing I knew to do was keep doing what I'd been doing all along: praying, availing myself of the Sacraments, participating in the fellowship of sober alcoholic brothers and sisters that, day after day, saved my life. The only thing I knew to do was keep walking, hand-in-hand with Christ, through the dark wood.

Who better to walk with than the little saint who had offered herself as a "holocaust victim" to love? Who better to guide me through this thicket than the Little Flower who from childhood had given up all earthly love in favor of a greater love? I could bring Thérèse with me to Mass. I could walk with Thérèse on my daily rounds through my L.A. neighborhood of Koreatown: to the Assi grocery store, the Benitez produce truck, 24-Hour Fitness, the Pio-Pico branch library. I could bring her with me while working at my desk, while driving the freeways, in my interactions with family, strangers, adversaries, and friends. Thérèse could show me how to continue to steer my own course. She could demonstrate how to get to the love, because love was her vocation.

Thérèse was attractive for one further reason: she was a memoirist who wrote of the spiritual path. She could shed light on the vitally important work of bringing beauty and richness, complexity, depth, and truth to the arts. She could especially guide those of us who were trying to tell the story of our ongoing journey to Christ.

The world tells us to strive for fame: Thérèse strove to be forgotten. The world rewards passing things: Thérèse strove for eternity. I, too, wanted to glorify God. I, too, wanted to leave writing that endured. I was willing to spend a year to read about, reflect upon, pray, eat, sleep, and live with a saint. I looked to St. Thérèse of Lisieux for help.

A Year with
Saint Thérèse of Lisieux

SHIRT *of* FLAME

—— JANUARY ——

EARLY LOSS

(On Facing Ancient Grievances)

I don't remember crying a lot; I didn't talk to anyone about the deep feelings I was experiencing. . . . I watched and listened in silence. . . .Nobody had the time to be concerned with me, so I saw lots of things that they might have wanted to keep hidden from me. Once, I found myself standing in front of the coffin lid. . . I stopped and considered it for a long time. I had never seen anything like it, but nevertheless I understood. . . .

—*The Story of a Soul* [p. 25]

THÉRÈSE'S FAMILY WAS DEEPLY RELIGIOUS—so religious, in fact, that her father Louis Martin, thirty-five at the time of his wedding, had initially proposed a celibate marriage. He and his wife, Zélie, went on to have nine children, three of whom died in infancy, a daughter who died at the age of five, and the five daughters who lived: Marie, Pauline, Léonie, Céline, and the baby, Thérèse, born on January 2, 1873.

In their hometown of Alençon, France, both parents attended 5:30 AM Mass daily. The family prayed and observed Holy Days together. While Zélie tended to her lace-making business, Louis, a jeweler, quoted the Gospels, took frequent pilgrimages, and refused to open his shop on Sundays, though that practice meant a loss of revenue. With her high spirits and blond curls, Thérèse was the unofficial favorite of the family. Her early childhood was happy. She was showered with affection. She was impish. She had "funny adventures" [SS, p. 8]. Her mother noted in a letter, "She's a child who gets easily emotional. As soon as some bad little thing happens to her, the whole world has to know about it" [SS, p. 9]. She revered her four sisters, and quickly became inseparable from Céline, the next oldest.

Thérèse left letters, poems, and plays as well, but her autobiography, *The Story of a Soul,* remains her definitive text. Of her childhood she wrote: "All my life it pleased the Good Lord to surround me with *love*. My earliest memories are imprinted with smiles and the most tender of embraces!. . . . I loved Papa and Mama very much, and showed them my tenderness in a thousand ways, because I was very expansive" [SS, p. 15].

She recounted the well-known "I choose all!" story:

One day Léonie, thinking she was now too big to play with dolls, came and found us both with a basket full of dresses and pretty little pieces of cloth intended to make others; on top was sitting her doll. "Here, little sisters," she said, "you *choose*, I'm giving you all this." Céline stuck out her hand and took a little ball of yarn that she liked. After thinking about it for a moment, I in turn stuck in my hand and said, "*I choose all!*" And I took the basket without further ceremony. [SS, p. 19]

The significance of the incident went far beyond a basket of fabric trimmings. "This childhood trait sums up my whole life," she wrote from the vantage point of adulthood. "Later, when perfection made its appearance to me, I understood that in order to become a saint you have to suffer a lot, always be in search of what is most perfect, and forget yourself" [*SS*, p. 19].

Thérèse didn't so much want all for herself as to give all of herself to God: "I don't want to be a *halfway saint*. It doesn't scare me to suffer for You; I'm afraid of only one thing, and that is to hold onto my *will*. Take it, because '*I choose all,*' all that You want!" [*SS*, p. 20].

She would soon have a chance to give perhaps more than she wanted. Because while those first years were idyllic, tragedy struck early: to wit, when Thérèse was just four and a half, her mother died of breast cancer. The event, naturally, marked a cataclysmic divide: "In the story of my soul up to my entrance into Carmel I distinguish three very different periods. The first, in spite of its shortness, is not the least fruitful in memories: It extends from the awakening of my reason, up to the departure of our dear mother to the homeland of heaven" [*SS*, p. 6].

No child ever fully recovers from the early death of a mother, and a soul as sensitive as Thérèse's was bound to almost fatally, if temporarily, wither. In fact, Zélie's death marked the beginning of what Thérèse called:

> . . . the second period of my existence, the most painful of the three. . . . This period stretches from the age of four and a half until my fourteenth year, the period when

I found my character as a *child* again, while yet entering
into the seriousness of [convent] life. . . .[S]tarting with
Mama's death, my happy character changed completely.
I, who had been so lively, so expansive, became timid
and mild, sensitive to excess. One look was enough to
make me burst into tears. I was happy only when nobody
was bothering with me. I couldn't stand the company of
strangers. . . . [*SS*, pp. 26–27]

Thus began the "crucible of outward and inward trials" [*SS*,
p. 4] in which this remarkable soul was formed and eventually
ripened. Thérèse was forever overly sensitive. She would
struggle with highly strung nerves for the rest of her life. But
perhaps the true sign of her character was this: though she
took the full measure of the hurt, after describing the incident
early in *The Story of a Soul,* she never again referred in her
autobiography to, nor by all accounts outwardly dwelt upon
this devastating loss.

Even as a child, Thérèse seemed to have looked inward for
solace. She seemed to have understood from the beginning that
life is a series of losses. She seemed instinctively to understand
that the love of God does not protect us from separation, illness,
grief, diminished family members, dysfunction, or death.

My own spiritual path, by contrast, had been a long, tortuous
journey of not so much giving all to God as having things
progressively wrested from me: my drinking, my career as a
lawyer, my marriage, my illusion that if only I sufficiently

managed and controlled, I could wrest satisfaction from life. Only recently had I begun to learn what Thérèse knew at four and a half—that no matter how far in the spiritual life we progress, we can't save anyone else. We couldn't have saved our siblings, our children, or our parents and, as we continue to meditate on Thérèse, we see that *they couldn't have saved us.*

This was a useful reflection as my own mother was still alive, back in New Hampshire, and I'd be lying if I said my feelings toward her were entirely unconflicted. She had given me so much!—a contemplative bent, a love for music and books—but Mom was hardly demonstrative, and I'm mortified to admit that I was *still* miffed because she'd never told me as a child (or an adult, for that matter) that I was pretty. Imagine my surprise to discover that Thérèse had received no compliments, either: not from her mother; not, after her mother died, from her nonetheless loving and attentive sisters. "You gave a lot of attention, dear Mother," she observed as an adult to Pauline, "not to let me near anything that might tarnish my innocence, especially not to let me hear a single word that might be capable of letting vanity slip into my heart" [*SS*, p. 46].

I'd never considered that not having received compliments might have been a gift. I'd never considered that learning to muddle through alone, without validation, had served me well: as a human being, as a writer. Just so, if we're 1) reading; 2) any book; and 3) especially a book about St. Thérèse of Lisieux, chances are that no matter how much we've suffered, we've also had enough to eat, we have a roof over our heads, and somebody, somewhere along the line, has done right by us.

Chances are that most of us are also still a teensy bit conflicted about our loved ones. Perhaps we're holding a grudge against a father who, say, never quite trusted us, or a narcissistically self-absorbed mother. Thérèse's whole spiritual life was built on the fact that, in spite of her early loss she'd been doted upon, embraced, treasured as a child. What of the rest of us who, for whatever reason, have never felt especially treasured? What of those of us who instead feel a lifelong lack, a fretful craving? Thérèse demonstrates that the point isn't so much what happened in our childhoods as what we choose to do with them: after all, many children have been treasured as she was but have not gone on to attain sainthood. Many have suffered as she did and become not more loving, but more bitter.

Thérèse's gift was to have suffered early loss but to also have chosen to remain childlike. Not child*ish*, for from a very young age she was mature beyond her years, but child*like*: trusting, resilient, lost in wonder:

> I don't know if I've already talked to you about my love of snow. . . . When I was quite little, its whiteness used to delight me. . . . Where did I get this liking of snow? . . . .Perhaps from the fact that being a *little winter flower*, [having been born in January], the first covering with which my child's eyes saw nature embellished must have been its white coat. [*SS*, pp. 174–75]

[Jesus] sent me in profusion sheaves of cornflowers, big daisies, poppies, etc., all the flowers that delight me the most. There was even a little flower called a corn-cockle. . . . [*SS*, p. 199]

The contrast between the child who could swoon at a flower, and who would soon also long to shed her blood to the last drop for Christ is compelling. As spiritual writer Ronald Rolheiser puts it:

Thérèse of Lisieux fascinates us, and has a rare power to truly and healthily fire both our religious and our romantic imaginations, for three interpenetrating reasons: i) She is a child mystic, the Anne Frank of the spiritual life; ii) she is a woman of extraordinary paradox and complexity; and iii) she has that rare power to touch that previously touched part inside of us.

That "previously touched part" has been touched by Christ, in what Rolheiser goes on to call our "moral soul":

Inside of each of us there is a part [of] our being that might be called our moral soul. It is that place where we feel most strongly about the right and wrong of things and where all that is most precious to us is cherished, guarded, and held. It is also the place that feels violated when it is not sufficiently honoured and respected. It is in this deep inner place that we, ultimately, feel most alone. More deeply than we long for a sexual partner, we long for moral affinity, for someone to visit us in that deep part of ourselves where all that is most precious to us is cherished and guarded. Our deepest longing is for someone to sleep with morally. This is particularly true for very sensitive souls.

Thérèse, of course, was one such soul. Many of us similarly sensitive types tend, when hurt, to shut down; to erect an impenetrable fortress. We will not be so gullible again, we tell ourselves. The world will not walk over us. We will not be chumps. To choose not to shut down, but to open yet further, takes tremendous purity of heart. To choose to remain vulnerable, knowing that vulnerability inevitably invites further suffering, takes tremendous courage. Inside or outside of convent walls, we are all liable to undergo bereavement, tragedy, or spiritual crisis at any time. We cannot change the natural order. What we can do is change the attitude with which we live and die in it.

Gazing at a statue of Mary a month before her death, Thérèse mused, "Who could ever invent the Blessed Virgin?" Maybe in a way she was saying that in Mary, we have an über mother. Maybe she was saying that the Holy Family is an archetype for the family we long for, and that very few of us quite have. Maybe she was saying that the Crucifixion consists, in a way, in offering up our childhood wounds in order to die to our old selves and be born anew.

Whether those wounds consist of loss, hurt, sorrow, anger, of grief, neglect, abuse, or abandonment, the operative fact is that everyone else suffers from some combination of them, too. We can be grateful for the time we did have with the people who raised us. We can give thanks for all that we received and acknowledge all that we still lack. We can discover that of the rough material we've been given, every single thread of what we'll eventually contribute back to the tapestry of all humanity is every bit as important, needed, wanted, and cherished as every and any other scrap and thread.

We might never get to tie up all the loose ends, but we get to gather around the table, break out the food, laugh, tell stories, and share what we've been given anyway.

PRAYER

Lord, help us to remember that the accidents of our birth, family, upbringing are just that: accidents irrelevant to our essential worthiness and lovability.

Help us to see the crust of anger and hurt with which we try to protect ourselves from the world.

Help us not to be at such pains to fix everything, to bring everything into "wholeness" and "health," to exterminate in us all that is broken and weak.

Help us to remember that we can comfort each other simply by being who we are at any given moment.

Help us to remember that just as Thérèse chose every last bit of ribbon and thread, you choose all of us.

THE CONFLUENCE OF WILL AND GRACE

(On Illness and Healing)

It is impossible to write a book about psychological suffering in any form, without referring again and again to Teresa Martin. . . . At eight years old Teresa fell ill with what was unquestionably a neurotic illness and was baffling to the doctors of her day. . . . There were certainly natural causes for the curious illness, but there was also the supernatural one—that no one could better offer the burden of psychological suffering than this really good child: no one could sanctify the feeling of guilt better than she. She was preparing for our generation.

—CARYLL HOUSELANDER

AS I SANK INTO THE LIFE AND WRITINGS of Thérèse, I began to realize how inadequate I felt to "walk" with a saint. How could a mortal soul such as myself—fallen, petty, impatient—hope to plumb the thought of a Doctor of the Church? How could a citizen of twenty-first-century Los Angeles find common ground with a nineteenth-century cloistered French nun? Yet, I hadn't been drawn to this particular saint by chance. I, too, was on fire for Christ. I, too, struggled to know what it meant to give fully of myself as a woman. And I, too, had known psychological suffering and neurotic illness.

Soon after Zélie's death, Monsieur Martin moved his five daughters from Alençon to the Lower Normandy town of Lisieux, the home of Thérèse's maternal aunt, uncle, and cousins, the Guérins. Here, "Every afternoon I would go on a little walk with Papa. We would go visit the Blessed Sacrament, visiting a different church each day. . . . I used to love the country, the flowers, and the birds so much! . . . Then my thoughts were very deep, and without knowing what it meant to meditate, my soul would plunge into real prayer" [SS, pp. 29–30].

Thérèse immediately settled upon Pauline, the second eldest daughter, as her new "Mama." Céline chose the eldest, Marie. (Léonie, the middle child, who suffered from eczema, threw tantrums, and is invariably described as "troublesome," apparently, and sadly, went without a new "Mama"). For a time, Thérèse's older sisters taught her at home. But when Thérèse was eight and a half, Léonie left school at the nearby Benedictine abbey and Thérèse took her place. Naturally intelligent, and having received excellent homeschooling, Thérèse proved to be the most advanced pupil of her age. She wanted to make the most of the experience—her first outside the sheltered environment of home—and when the older, rougher girls rebuffed her friendly overtures, she was stung. She never confided her troubles to the people at home, but her outsider status and her continuing inability to fit in made her miserable:

I've often heard that time spent at school is the best and the sweetest time of life. That's not how it was for me; the five years I spent there were the saddest of my life. If I hadn't had my dear Céline [the youngest of my sisters, three and a half years older than I] with me, I wouldn't have been able to stay a single month without falling sick. . . . [*SS*, p. 47]

School imparted a sense of exile, and so, all too soon, did home. Eventually, all five of the Martin sisters would become cloistered nuns.[1] The first to leave, in 1882 for the convent at Carmel, was Pauline—the sister Thérèse adored and looked up to as a second mother. So close were the two that Thérèse had assumed they would go out into the world as spiritual pilgrims together. "One day, I had told Pauline that I would like to be a hermit and go away with her to a faraway deserted place. She answered that the desire was hers as well, and that she *would wait* until I was big enough to leave" [*SS*, p. 54].

But Pauline did not wait. And though the separation would have been painful under any circumstances, the way Thérèse learned of it—by overhearing a conversation between Pauline and Marie—proved to be peculiarly devastating: "If I had learned in a gentle way about my beloved Pauline's departure, perhaps I wouldn't have suffered so much, but

---

[1] Pauline in 1882, then Marie in 1886, both to Carmel; followed by Léonie, originally to the Poor Clares in 1886, and after a series of failed attempts, to the nearby Visitation convent in 1899, where she remained until her death; then Thérèse in 1888, and finally Céline, in 1894, both to Carmel.

since I learned it by surprise, I felt as if a sword had been thrust into my heart (Lk. 2:35)" [SS, p. 55]. For the second time in a very short life, the ground had been removed from beneath Thérèse's feet. "In an instant I understood what life was . . . I saw that it was only suffering and continual separation" [SS, pp. 54–55].

The shock of the cloister doors' forever closing behind Pauline so completely overwhelmed Thérèse that she soon became emotionally and spiritually ill: "It's surprising to see how much my mind developed in the midst of suffering. It developed to such a point that it didn't take me long to fall sick" [SS, p. 58].

The sickness dragged on for six weeks and took the form of a "strange trembling," hyperventilation, hallucinations, and agitation so extreme that Thérèse took to hurling herself with frighteningly violent force against the walls of her bedroom. Commentators have variously ascribed the illness to St. Vitus's Dance, the early effects of tuberculosis, or sexual hysteria: in retrospect, Thérèse herself viewed the affliction as a kind of possession: "The illness that struck me came most certainly from the devil, who was furious at [Pauline's] entry into Carmel. He wanted to take revenge on me for the wrong that our family was to do to him in the future" [SS, p. 58].

It's been said that an age that doesn't believe in miracles doesn't believe in evil. Thérèse believed in both. "A *miracle* was needed" [SS, p. 64], and a miracle occurred. One Sunday, Marie, Céline, and Léonie knelt by Thérèse's bed, turned toward a statue of the Blessed Virgin Mary and, along with Thérèse, offered their most fervent prayers:

> Suddenly the Blessed Virgin seemed *beautiful* to me, *so beautiful* that I had never seen anything so beautiful. Her face was breathing inexpressible goodness and tenderness, but what penetrated right to the depths of my soul was the "lovely smile of the Blessed Virgin." . . . Oh! I thought, the Blessed Virgin smiled at me, how happy I am. . . . Yes, but I will never tell anyone about it, because then my *happiness would disappear*. [*SS*, p. 65]

Eventually, she was forced to tell. When Marie asked for permission to inform the Carmelites of the event, Thérèse, obedient to a fault, couldn't say no. She was made to stand in front of the nuns and answer questions that "troubled me and gave me a lot of distress"—"Marie asked me if the Blessed Virgin was carrying the baby Jesus, or if there was a lot of light and so on" [*SS*, p. 67]—questions that tend to be asked by people who are more interested in the paranormal than in the mystical. That Thérèse answered them so patiently, in spite of her misgivings, is a testament to the high development of her character even at this very early age.

The literature on St. Thérèse is voluminous. There are hagiographies. There are revisionists. There are those who exalt, those who attempt to tear down, and those who try to make Thérèse into something other than or different from human. But one book no serious student of Thérèse should miss is *The Hidden Face*, by Ida Friederike Görres. With penetrating sympathy, acute intelligence, and brilliant psychospiritual insight, Görres delves deep to posit the innermost workings of Thérèse's soul.

Here is Görres's description, for example, of what might have happened beneath the level of consciousness to effect Thérèse's cure:

> [S]he could abandon her wild despair over what she had lost, could really carry out the unendurable renunciation within the core of her ego, could release the hand of Pauline and reach across the irrevocable gulf for the hand of the Blessed Virgin. Or—and this was the other possibility—she could cling to her despair, could hold tight to her neurosis, could maintain her protest, stubbornly persist at all costs in the sinister attempt at blackmail which this disease represented. Such decisions take place not by deliberate processes of thought, but far below the strata of thoughts and words, by a lightning-like opening or closing of the core of being.

Thérèse may not have been brought to a spiritual crisis in the particular way I had been—through alcoholism—but she *had* been brought to a crisis by a "neurotic illness": her hypersensitivity, her inability to put the desire to please God before the desire to be noticed, coddled, and loved, which—along with the neurological glitch that gives rise to the phenomenon of craving and the "allergic" response that gives rise to mental obsession—is really what alcoholism consists of.

Görres's description of the lightning-quick opening that takes place below the strata of consciousness paralleled the "yes" I'd given to getting sober: a consent to grow up, take on the responsibilities of adulthood, and orient my life toward service. I may never have had a vision of the Virgin Mary, but I had come to know that the problem was not the world, but me. I may not have entered the convent, but I had found much healing in a fellowship of brother and sister alcoholics who were trying to stay sober. That the solution to a compulsion that had very nearly killed me, in fact, had turned out to be communing with a bunch of other ex-addicts and drunks— examining our blackened consciences, trying to make things right with the people we'd hurt, cracking jokes—told me almost everything I "knew" about God.

As an alcoholic, I'd always been interested in the mind-body connection, in the way God sometimes seems to take us "out of the world" for a period of time, possibly in order to work on our subconscious. I, too, had experienced situations from which there seemed to be no escape. I, too, had been in the grip of a kind of dark night that seemed impervious to all reason, all human help, all prayer. Grace is needed and yet grace also seems most likely to appear—as had happened in my case— when, from the depths of our heart we cry out our misery and ask for help. Most likely, perhaps, but not inevitably: in fact, the seeming randomness of who gets out from beneath the obsession for alcohol and who doesn't; who stays sober for decades and who dies in the gutter, makes this confluence of will and grace one of the deepest mysteries I know.

For in the end, what else except grace can explain when, why, and that we are ever saved from our compulsions, obsessions, and neuroses? Why does one incest victim become a pathological hoarder and another open a clinic to counsel other incest victims? Why does one person end up in the psych ward and another channel her nervous energy into composing music? Why was Thérèse delivered and not the hundreds of thousands of others who have prayed to the Virgin Mary for healing?

We don't know. We can only be grateful when and if the lightning-quick opening occurs. We can only know that we are not loved one iota more if we get sober, or one iota less if we stay drunk. We can only hope to do the best we can with what we've been given. We can only understand that the opening is an incipient yes to a lifetime of hard inner work. And we can accept as well that the yes—transformative though the effect may be at the time—doesn't protect us from further troubles.

The crisis of the neurotic illness was over. On May 8, 1884, at the age of eleven, Thérèse made her First Communion. But the suffering continued, for, inexplicably coming to believe that she had *caused* the illness, Thérèse now proceeded to blame herself: "[F]or a long time after I got well I thought that I had become sick on purpose, and that was a *true martyrdom* for my soul" [*SS*, p. 61]. Then, at a retreat before her Second Communion, the abbé spoke of God's hatred of a soul in mortal sin. At thirteen, Thérèse, terrified, was plunged into the state of hyperguilt known as *scruples*.

Already given to keeping lists of penances, sacrifices, and prayers in a little notebook, she now very nearly exhibited signs of obsessive-compulsive disorder:

"It would be impossible for me to say what I suffered *for a year and a half* . . . All my thoughts and my simplest actions became a subject of trouble for me" [*SS*, p. 88].

She fretted endlessly about Confession. She feared offending God. "What patience didn't my dear Marie have to have, to listen to me without ever showing annoyance! . . . Scarcely had I come back from the Abbey when she began to curl my hair for the next day. . . . While my hair was being curled I couldn't stop crying as I told all my scruples" [*SS*, p. 88].

I never suffered from scruples—I should probably have more scruples—but I had certainly suffered many times from a fixed idea that bore little or no relation to reality and that I was powerless to cure myself: that I could manage and control my drinking, that the way to financial security was to hoard money, that I could "get" certain people to love me if only I loved *them* in some esoteric, magic-formula way.

Marie helped Thérèse to overcome her scruples by emphasizing that God is loving, indulgent, and merciful. Finally, however, Thérèse found the best solution herself: she spoke to her siblings who had died in infancy or young childhood—the "four little angels" who had gone to heaven before her:

> I thought that those innocent souls who had never known trouble or fear must surely have pity on their poor little

sister, who was suffering on earth. I talked to them with
the simplicity of a child. . . . Soon peace came and flooded
my soul with its delicious waves, and I understood that if
I was loved on earth, I was also loved in heaven. [SS, pp.
99–100]

To have an obsession, or a fear, or a blot on the conscience
that we can't let go of no matter how much inner work we do,
no matter how many moral inventories, no matter how many
times we go to Confession or write in our journals or talk to
our spiritual directors, is a special kind of suffering. But what's
really special is the idea of appealing for help not to those who
are stronger than us—but to those who are weaker.

Along with Thérèse, then, we can pray with those who
have no one to pray for them, with the children who died in
infancy, with those who died in the drunk tank, with those
who never had a chance to understand that they were "loved
in heaven." For to not feel loved, or useful, has to be the root
of all neuroses—particularly the neuroses of the modern age,
with its technology, its dehumanizing speed, its profound
sense of existential exile—and by asking those weaker than
us for help, and praying for them as well, we close the circle
in a new way.

If Thérèse is the saint of our age, maybe one of the things
she is saying most clearly is that Christ is the way, not of
rewards and triumphs, but of mystery and paradox: that we're
"healed" not to revel in victory, but to develop compassion, to
help bear the burden of those who are still suffering.

Maybe, in fact, we need to revise our idea of healing. Maybe the people who are never healed, who carry the almost unbearable tension of wanting to get sober but not being able to—of wanting the neurotic illness to end, but of the illness not ending—are the ones who keep the world spinning on its axis. Maybe the fact that we pray at all is itself the answer to prayer. Maybe the deepest desire of our hearts is simply to turn toward God, whether or not we ever "hear" an answer. Maybe the most we can do is prepare ourselves to be open to grace—by prayer, the Sacraments, and works of mercy—even though we sometimes feel those things aren't helping us or anyone else at all.

PRAYER

For those of us whose minds tend to run in obsessive ruts,
For those of us with the impulse to manage and control,
For those of us who can't stop taking our emotional temperature,
For those of us who tend to hoard money and love,
For those of us who think we know best,
For those of us who tend to strive for straight A's on some cosmic report card,
For those of us who are disciplined, sometimes to a fault,
For those of us who have difficulty forgiving ourselves and difficulty forgiving others,
For those who didn't make it—
St. Thérèse, pray for us.

THÉRÈSE'S SECOND CONVERSION

(On Learning to Serve)

Thérèse could pour out bucketfuls of reverential tears; she had seen the heavens open and the smile of the Blessed Virgin. But she could not, simply *could not*, manage what the most average, worldly, and superficial of her fellow pupils managed without any difficulty: to accept a harsh word unperturbed, smile in the face of mockery or reproach, master her feelings at receiving a poor mark.

—IDA FRIEDERIKE GÖRRES

HERE WAS ONE PLACE I WAS JUST LIKE THÉRÈSE, or Thérèse as a prepubescent child: her habit of melodramatically over-emoting:

I was really unbearable due to my overly great sensitivity. So if it happened that I involuntarily gave a slight amount of trouble to a person I loved, instead of taking the high road and *not crying,* I increased my fault, instead of reducing it, by *crying* like a baby. And when I started to become comforted by the thing itself, I *cried because I had cried.* . . . All this reasoning was useless, and I couldn't manage to correct this wicked fault. [*SS*, p. 102]

This hypersensitivity—which, if my own experience is any indication, in all fairness springs from an almost unimaginably deep hunger for connection—applied especially to her relationships with people. One of the most revealing incidents of Thérèse's childhood, in fact, was her feeling for, and rejection by, two of her classmates:

> My sensitive and loving heart would have easily given itself away if it had found another heart capable of understanding it. . . . I tried to link up with other little girls my age, especially with two of them. I loved them, and for their part they loved me as much as they were *capable* of loving. But alas! How *narrow and flighty* is the heart of created beings!!! . . . Soon I saw that my love wasn't understood.
>
> One of my girlfriends, who had been obliged to go back home to her family, came back several months later. During her absence I had *thought about her*, carefully guarding a little ring that she had given me. My joy was great when I saw my friend again, but alas! All I got was an indifferent look. [*SS*, p. 85]

What today we call "love addiction" was in medieval times referred to as "attachment," from old European roots meaning *nailed to*. I'm not suggesting that Thérèse's attachment to her friend was pathological, but I am suggesting that the mark of the saint is an extreme capacity for love: "I recognize that without Him, I would have fallen as low as Mary Magdalene did" [*SS*, p. 86]. I am suggesting that Thérèse herself recognized that only grace kept these and similar fever-pitch feelings from leading her astray. (Years afterward in the convent she would conceive for a time a kind of crush on her superior, Mother Marie de Gonzague, suffering such torments when she passed by Mother's room that she had to clutch the banister in order to restrain herself from looking in for a kind word or an affectionate glance.)

While today people tend to view similarly intense feelings as a sign of the need for psychotherapy, Thérèse discovered contemplation:

> One day one of my teachers at the Abbey school asked me what I did on my days off when I was alone. I replied that I would go behind my bed into an empty space that was there and that was easy for me to shut off with the curtain, and there, *I would think*. "But what do you think about?" she said. "I think about God, about life . . . about ETERNITY, I just *think*!" [*SS*, p. 74]

And while most girls hunger, as they approach puberty, for a flesh-and-blood boy, Thérèse increasingly hungered for the one thing higher: the real Body and Blood of Christ: "How I thank Jesus for making me find only bitterness in the friendships of this world," she wrote. "With a heart like mine, I would have let myself be taken and my wings clipped, and then how would I have been able to fly away and find rest? How can a heart that is given over to the affection of created beings be intimately united with God?" [SS, p. 85].

The conviction that if only the particular created being I had in my sights would respond the way I wanted him to, I'd be happy, went back for me to about the age of twelve. I'd always been dazzled by male beauty. I'd always tended to forget to worship the Creator, not the created. The same intense spiritual hunger had driven both my drinking and my tendency to romantically obsess; in fact, my whole dodgy career at the bars had been inextricably bound up with my search for the One. If the latest attachment had been by far the most volatile, the most painful, and the longest-lived, the good news was that I also knew I'd been undergoing—had to undergo—a massive psychic death in order to free myself for a more mature way to love, romantic or otherwise.

Sooner or later, everyone on a serious spiritual path has to undergo such a death. Because loving someone who doesn't or can't love us back is a theme with many variations. Perhaps our child has married someone we don't care for. Perhaps our spouse is lost to drugs or alcohol or extramarital sex. Perhaps we've done everything we can to make peace with an old wound, and the wound refuses to heal. The inability to put the desire to seek God's will before the desire to be noticed, accommodated, and coddled was a real stumbling block for Thérèse as well, and she knew it.

At the age of thirteen, she underwent what she called her "second conversion" around this very issue. The French custom on Christmas Eve at the time was for the children of the house to leave their shoes by the fireplace for the parents to fill with candy. As the youngest of the Martin daughters, Thérèse was the last to keep up the ritual. Returning from the vigil Mass that night in 1886, her father, tired and uncharacteristically cranky, passed the pair of filled shoes and remarked: "Well, fortunately this is the last year." Thérèse overheard and ran upstairs, ostensibly to take off her hat. Her impulse was to burst into tears and make a scene, as she would in the past. Instead, she paused halfway up the stairs, willed herself to smile, turned around, marched back to the parlor, embraced her father and opened her gifts with joy, good cheer, and thanks.

The episode marked a turning point: the entry into the third, and what would be by far the most fruitful, portion of her spiritual life:

> In an instant, the work that I hadn't been able to do in ten years—Jesus did it. . . . On that *night of light* the third period of my life began, the most beautiful of them all, the most filled with graces from heaven. . . . I felt a great desire to work for the conversion of sinners, a desire that I had never felt so strongly. . . . In a word, I felt *charity* enter into my heart, the need to forget myself in order to please others, and ever afterward I was happy! [*SS*, p. 104]

This movement from the immature, fretful craving to have things the way we want them, to the way that is patient, cheerful, nonobtrusive, and oriented toward others, is a true death: the death of our egos, the death of our identities as people who respond—can only respond—a certain way. Grace is needed, to be sure, but preparing the ground for continuing grace requires prayer, meditation, and consenting to the long, hard work of pruning our will in such a way that we are open to maturity.

We have to acknowledge that we get something out of holding on to old hurts; out of the grandiosity that makes us and our emotions the center of the universe. We tell ourselves we're giving when we're really imposing. We tell ourselves we're being passionate when we're really being possessive. We tell ourselves we're loving people when we're really trying to manipulate them into loving us.

Dante scholar and Jungian psychologist Helen M. Luke charts the hero's journey in which we women in particular are called to surrender our deepest desires for affection, companionship, and emotional security:

> [The woman] will need great courage if she is to recognize and confront the half-conscious plotting and scheming of the animus in order to get her own way or to prove herself in the right. Thus she enters on the quest for her true identity as an individual woman. The way will bring her into darkness and loneliness, through fire and water, but at the last she will begin to discover consciously that unpossessive love between persons which brings renewal of faith in life itself and finally the *agape* of wholeness.

The "*agape* of wholeness" never means being indifferent or cold; it simply means walking our own paths while leaving our loved ones to theirs. *Agape* means that we refrain from projecting our unworked-through issues upon the folks around us. *Agape* means loving people for the simple fact that they exist. In fact, fully living his own life, and giving with no expectation of return, was the way that Christ conducted *all* his relationships.

What Thérèse accomplished at the age of thirteen—halfway up the staircase of her childhood home—takes many of us well into middle or even older age. Dante's *The Divine Comedy*— the classic poetic work charting the journey from immature to mature love—also took place on a kind of elaborately allegorical staircase: from hell to purgatory to heaven.

But on the earthly plane the ascension into paradise seems to begin in just such homely acts as putting on a good face and pretending to enjoy the Christmas candy. Someone breaks a lunch date to which we'd been looking forward for weeks. Instead of showing we're hurt, we can say, "I'd so still love to see you! When can we reschedule?" A friend inadvertently upstages our birthday party with the announcement of her pregnancy: we take a bit of a back seat and rejoice for her with the rest of the guests. That's not dishonesty; that's maturity. That's refraining from making every little thing about us. That's caring about the spiritual well-being of the other. That's wearing the world like a loose garment.

And make no mistake, such seemingly insignificant actions hurt. Here's Helen M. Luke again:

[T]o give up a misery . . . is to deprive the ego of one of its main sources of nourishment. . . . In order to feel meaningful, the old self must always be either dramatically weak and miserable, or dramatically strong and unselfish, busily helping the weak and miserable and deciding what is right for them. . . . The "new self," on the other hand, will, when in misery, ask for help with simple acceptance and willingness to let go no matter how empty he may feel; or . . . he will give of himself without any sense of being thereby increased in significance.

The way to become whole, in other words, is to become most fully ourselves—a lifelong task that paradoxically requires us to rub up against, be filed down by, cracked open by, and perhaps most unexpectedly of all, loved by the very people whom we wish to serve. We can't cloister ourselves out of fear of relationships—as Thérèse certainly did not—but we do need to offer up our ideas of whether and in what way people "should" love us.

Whether the people in question are our parents, our spouses, our employees, our friends, or those to whom we're emotionally or romantically drawn, Thérèse wasn't saying that we have to choose between God and a flesh-and-blood person. She was saying that focusing on ourselves and our relationship with God is the way that we come to feel truly loved, which is what we've wanted all along—and what so many of us spend way too much of our lives trying to get from a human being.

PRAYER

Lord, help me to act mature when my heart is breaking.

Lord, help me to be loving when I'm afraid that there won't be enough love for me.

Lord, help me to remember that you are the source of all true affection, companionship, and emotional security.

Lord, help me to let go of all hope that a person, place, or thing can fix me.

Lord, help me not to show when my feelings are hurt.

Lord, save me from pouting, giving the silent treatment, and showing scorn.

Lord, help me to grow up.

Lord, help me to serve.

— APRIL —

THE PAPAL VISIT

(On Daring to Ask)

No doubt, those three privileges are my vocation—
Carmelite, Bride, and Mother—but I feel within myself
other vocations. I feel the vocation of Warrior, Priest,
Apostle, Teacher, Martyr. In short, I feel the need and the
desire to accomplish for You, Jesus, all the most heroic
works. . . . I feel in my soul the courage of a Crusader, of
a soldier in the papal army; I would like to die on a field
of battle in defense of the Church. . . . But above all, my
Beloved Savior, I would like to shed my blood for You
until the last drop.

—*The Story of a Soul* [pp. 214–15]

PAULINE ENTERED THE CLOISTER in 1882. In 1886, Marie
also left for Carmel. The middle daughter, Léonie, likewise
embarked upon the first of many attempts at life as a nun that
year (in 1899 she would enter the Visitation convent and remain
until her death).

By 1887, the only remaining members of the Martin
household were thus Thérèse, Thérèse's next oldest sister,
Céline, to whom she remained extremely close, and their
father. At the age of fourteen Thérèse no longer attended

school at the Benedictine abbey, but twice a week she attended meetings there that would allow her to join a Catholic youth organization called the Sodality of the Children of Mary.

At this point in her story, we really begin to feel the loneliness of a soul who, her whole life, would have no emotional or spiritual peer:

> I didn't have, like the other former students, a *teacher friend* with whom I could go spend several hours. .. . Nobody paid attention to me, so I went up to the gallery of the chapel, and I remained before the Blessed Sacrament until the time when Papa would come to get me. This was my only comfort: Wasn't Jesus my *only Friend*? [*SS*, p. 91]

In our "confessional" culture folks routinely go on national TV to air their stories of incest, wife-beating, and compulsive overeating. But one thing no one much likes admitting to is loneliness. I'm not talking about the kind of loneliness that can be assuaged by socializing, work, or even the kindest and most devoted friends. I'm talking about the essential friendlessness of the human condition. I'm talking about the inevitable loneliness that comes with the attempt to follow Christ. To be a follower of Christ is necessarily to be out of step with a world that worships money, success, power, youth, and sex. We connect—with ourselves, with God, with each other—in the deepest possible way, but that doesn't necessarily translate into companionship, empathy, validation, daily support, or sometimes even a simple acknowledgment of our existence.

I wonder if Christ does not arrange things this way, so that even those of us who are sociable, who are often invited to participate, will suffer this deep loneliness in which we, too, find that Jesus is our "only Friend." I wonder whether, when the desire for Christ burns bright enough and hard enough, loneliness isn't the inevitable ash. I wonder whether to follow a Savior who subverts all power systems—social, political, economic, even familial—does not lead us into a kind of necessary and terrible exile.

One thing I do know: we tamp down that desire to our own detriment. Monsignor Lorenzo Albacete, priest, theologian, physicist, and author, shares a personal story about the spiritual peril that he calls "the reduction of desire."

A student was driving him to a university building, a residence for priests, where he was to spend the night. They arrived and he spotted a parking space in front of the residence with a sign "Reserved for Residents," which to his mind meant priest residents, however temporary. "Ah, parking right up front," he observed. But to his surprise and consternation, she drove right by and proceeded to a public parking lot that seemed to a person of his bulk to be several miles away!

Clearly the distance was not a problem for her—she was thin and small and could easily cover that distance—but it was for me.

I said, "Look, did you see that parking place back there?" She replied, "Yes, but that's for priest residents." And I said, "Wait a minute! Number one, we're just dropping off the luggage. Number two, I am a priest resident of this building tonight, so I have a right to it as a priest resident." I continued, "So I think we have a right to park there."

Monsignor Albacete acknowledged to himself that his argument might have stretched the point.

But what shocked me was that she wasn't even attracted by it! She had no desire to park nearby. I told her, "You suffer from the reduction of desire." Now my desire to park up front would be so great that I would look for the smallest justification in order to be able to do that. But she didn't even struggle with this. She didn't mind going miles away to park in the student lot. My driver's response to the parking situation is emblematic to me of the problem of the reduction of desire. She didn't park up front because the educational system, with its laws and punishments for breaking the law, had drilled into her that she should accept her spot as a student and not have ambition that might be beyond her rightful place in society. That is how power remains in power—by reducing our desire.

I find this story fascinating, not least of all because I so related to that rule-following driver. My Pharisee desire to get good spiritual marks would have led me to follow the parking sign to the letter. My Calvinistic streak would have primly thought: *Well you should just exercise more, Father.* [Disclaimer: I have had the great honor of meeting Msgr. Albacete and, like probably just everyone else who comes in contact with this holy, very funny man, instantly warmed to him.]

Msgr. Albacete's story leads me to reflect that maybe this is why we need suffering, and why we need love: because without one or the other of them to blow us apart, we will comply with the letter, rather than the spirit, of the law like sheep. We will suffer from a fatal reduction of desire. We will dumbly go along with the dictates of our culture; the not-always-entirely-devoid-of-ulterior-motive desires of our spouses, children, bosses, and friends; the powers and principalities of peer pressure and fear of ridicule; our perpetual human resistance to effort or change of any kind. Love is the wild card that gives us the incandescent drive to subvert all power systems. Desire is the unpredictable *x* that throws off all bets.

Thérèse suffered from many things, but reduction of desire was not one of them. Her own desire to enter the convent had been kindled when Pauline first left for Carmel and had only grown in the five years since. Now "the Divine call was so pressing that even if I had had to *pass through flames* I would have done so in order to be faithful to Jesus" [*SS*, p. 113].

Sitting before the Blessed Sacrament in the abbey chapel in the spring of 1887, she formed a private decision to enter Carmel that very year—on the first anniversary of her Christmas conversion. But what to do about her father, Louis, who had already lost three daughters to the cloister?

In June, she resolved to speak, and after Vespers one evening, she asked him to take a walk and told him of her plan.

The moment was defining. Tears ran down his face. He pointed out that Thérèse "was still quite young to make such a serious determination" [*SS*, p. 116]. Yet the stalwart Monsieur Martin nonetheless gave his consent, and in such a way that we well know from whom Thérèse inherited her famous charm: He plucked "some *little white flowers* that looked like miniature lilies, and taking one of those flowers, he gave it to me, explaining to me with what care God had caused it to grow and had preserved it until that day" [*SS*, p. 117].

Louis Martin may well have been putty in his daughter's hands, but I can't help thinking a certain law of the universe was also at work here: the law that says, "Ask, and it will be given you" (Matt. 7:7). The law that says, "For truly, I say to you, if you have faith as a grain of mustard seed, you will say to this mountain, 'Move hence to yonder place,' and it will move; and nothing will be impossible for you" (Matt. 17:20). The law that decrees once you believe something can happen, and do the footwork to invite the thing to happen, at least enough events fall into place to move you along to the next stage.

The first hurdle had been crossed. But while Thérèse's father had acquiesced, everyone else seemed to suddenly rise up to conspire against her: the parish priest; her uncle Isodore Guérin, who forbade her to even talk about her vocation until she was seventeen; and the Superior of Carmel, who would now not consent to Thérèse's entrance till the age of twenty-one.

Here arises yet another paradox in the soul of young Thérèse Martin. For while on the one hand Thérèse was ever pliant, obedient, and eager to please, throughout her life she also knew exactly what she wanted and went about attaining her goals with single-minded, utterly focused determination. She would have various confessors, for example, but never a spiritual director upon whom she relied completely, an office reserved for Jesus alone [*SS*, p. 172]. She had an extremely high—perhaps exalted—opinion of herself: on her deathbed she would tell her sisters, "You know well you are taking care of a little saint."

So what happened next was emblematic. Even at this early juncture Thérèse's vocation was so completely formed that she regarded the levels of authority arrayed against her and simply, calmly stared them down. She was so determined to enter Carmel that she soon decided to bypass her family, the parish priest, and the Mother Superior, take the Vatican by storm, and personally appeal to the Pope of the Roman Catholic Church: "I was resolved *to take this as far as necessary.* I even said that I would go to the *Holy Father,* [Pope Leo XIII himself,] if the bishop didn't want to allow me to enter Carmel at the age of fifteen" [*SS*, p. 122].

The bishop, it transpired, did not so desire and, true to her word, several months later Thérèse traveled, along with Céline, her father, and a larger group of pilgrims, to Rome. Here, too, as we read between the lines, Thérèse broke the rules at every turn. Visitors weren't allowed to enter the Coliseum, for instance, but she somehow managed to gate-crash, kneel on the sacred ground where the martyrs had fought, and kiss the "dust that was tinged with crimson by the blood of the first Christians" [SS, p. 146]. At the tomb of the virgin martyr St. Cecilia, she and Céline "slipped away" from the others and swiped "some of the earth that had been made holy by her presence" [SS, p. 147].

And at the church of St. Agnes, another virgin martyr, Thérèse longed for a relic, "[b]ut it was impossible for us to have anything but a little red stone that came loose from a rich mosaic. . . . Wasn't it charming that the lovable Saint herself would give us what we were looking for and that was forbidden to us to take?" [SS, p. 148]. Maybe, but "came loose" *how*? It's impossible not to imagine some very busy fourteen-year-old fingers helping that little red stone along.

No matter, for on November 20, 1887, Thérèse knelt at the feet of Pope Leo XIII and, in spite of having been given strict orders on no account to actually speak, pleaded: "Most Holy Father, I have a great grace to ask of you! . . . Most Holy Father, in honor of your jubilee, allow me to enter Carmel at the age of fifteen." The Pope, startled, responded, "Well, my child, do what your superiors tell you." At which point, not satisfied with that remark, Thérèse placed her hands on his knees and in a pleading voice begged, "'Oh! Most Holy Father, if you were to say yes, everyone would be willing!' . . . He looked at me fixedly and pronounced these words, emphasizing each syllable: 'All right . . . All right . . . *You will enter if it is God's will*'" [*SS*, pp. 151–52].

Still loath to leave without having received a definite yes, Thérèse was then taken by the arms by the Papal Guards, lifted up, and forcibly torn away, sobbing.

Disappointment, of a caliber seemingly calculated to end the world, is an experience with which I deeply identified. I might never have had to be torn away from the Vicar of Christ by the Papal Guard, but I had certainly known the emotional devastation of being romantically rejected. I had known the searing pain of having book manuscripts on which I'd worked for years fail to sell. In fact, I'd suffered so many disappointments in the preceding decade—divorce, the death of my beloved father, cancer, unrequited love, career setbacks—that I was no longer sure which way to turn. Was God himself playing hard to get? Had I fallen through the cracks completely, as I'd secretly feared since birth I would?

Thérèse responded to her own disappointment with a typical mixture of two seemingly opposite traits. The first was childlike transparency:

> For some time I had offered myself to the Child Jesus to be His *little toy* . . . a little ball of no value that He could throw on the ground, kick around, *pierce*, leave in a corner or press to His heart if that pleased Him. . . . In Rome Jesus *pierced* His little toy. He wanted to see what was inside it, and then, having seen it, content with His discovery,

He dropped His little ball and went to sleep. [*SS*, pp. 153–54]

The second was renewed, and ever-steelier, determination: the doors to Carmel might have been closed, but Thérèse continued for the next six months to push, pray, coax, cajole, and persevere.

Here's Dante scholar Helen M. Luke again:

> Disobedience to authority, *at the right moment*, is the essential of any and every breakthrough of new awareness; disobedience with a condition, however. It is senseless and meaningless rebellion if it is not inspired by a real devotion to a conscious value, and if there is not complete willing-ness at the same time to suffer the consequences, whatever they may be.

If love gives us the courage to subvert all power systems, in other words, then love is also the vehicle that enables us to discern in any given situation when restraint is called for and when boldness.

As much of a "people-pleaser" as I could sometimes be, when I'd quit my job as a lawyer fifteen years earlier to begin writing, I, too, had had an experience akin to Thérèse's. My own "disobedience to authority" had translated into this: "Yes, I'm deeply grateful to be sober and to have been supported by a job as a lawyer for a time, but it's not for me. I can't and won't do such work anymore, and if I have to be thought of as a quitter, disappoint my parents, bewilder my [now ex-] husband, and possibly become a bag lady, so be it—because I *must* write."

Thérèse, for her part, *had* to enter Carmel—and for all her devotion to and reverence for her family, let's not forget that her insistence on leaving home more or less broke her father's heart. That night in the garden he agreed to let her go, but had he balked, we sense that she would have forged ahead anyway, no matter what the cost.

Sooner or later on the spiritual path, in ways sometimes small and sometimes large, we all stand at such crossroads ourselves. Maybe our parents expect us to go one way, and we know in our hearts that we're called to go another. Maybe we're longing to propose marriage (or just ask someone on a date!), for a loan to buy a house, to move across the country, to change careers, to join a holy order. Whether the problem is pride, weary resignation, sloth, fear of incurring the displeasure of others, or fear of failure, we have to dare to ask—for the discernment, the courage, the permission, the impossible. We can't afford the reduction of desire. To refuse to ask is to think that we know the plan. To reduce our desire is to reduce God.

The point is that littleness in no way precludes fighting for our vocations, our callings, or the desires of our hearts. Littleness doesn't mean never getting what we want. Littleness arises from the conviction that we're supported, cherished, guided. Littleness gives rise to formidable resolve.

"Woman's will, God's will," the French say: Thérèse entered Carmel, at the age of fifteen, on April 9, 1888.

PRAYER

God, be with me in my loneliness.

God, give me the courage to stay the course.

God, lead me to the people who will help me to discern your will.

God, let me be willing to shed my blood to the last drop, even though most of the time I'm not willing to shed even one drop.

God, if I'm called to go against the wishes of those who are close to me, let me do so with humility and love.

God, grant me the serenity to accept the things I cannot change, the courage to change the things I can, and the wisdom to know the difference.

POVERTY, CHASTITY, OBEDIENCE

(On Radical Social Conscience)

Almighty God, Creator of Heaven and earth, the Supreme Governor of the World, and the Very glorious Virgin Mary, Queen of the heavenly Court, request the honor of your presence at the Marriage of their August Son, Jesus, King of kings and Lord of lords, with Miss Thérèse Martin, now Lady and Princess of the kingdoms brought by dowry by her Divine Bridegroom, namely, the Childhood of Jesus and His Passion, her titles of nobility being: of the Child Jesus and of the Holy Face.

—*The Story of a Soul* [p. 189]

I CAME OUT OF THE WOMB WEARING MY HEART on my sleeve. I am the sap of all saps. But even *I* sometimes cringed at Thérèse's over-amped emotional-aesthetic sensibility. Even I didn't use *quite* so many italics and caps. Even I'd read a passage such as, "I consider myself as a weak little bird covered only with a light down" [*SS*, p. 221], or, "Stay in me as you do in the tabernacle, and never leave this little host of yours," and wonder what Thérèse might have to say to the gang members in my neighborhood, to pregnant twelve-year-olds, to the one of every eighteen U.S. males who's behind bars or being monitored.

For all her flowery language, though, the way of St. Thérèse was the way of radical social conscience and radical martyrdom. Her mission, she strongly sensed, was to save souls, and in a well-known incident that occurred shortly after the "second conversion," she'd begun to pray for an unrepentant murderer named Pranzini who had been convicted of brutally killing two women and a child. At the same time, she had asked God for a sign. On his way to the guillotine on September 1, 1887, Pranzini had grabbed the crucifix a priest had been holding up to him and kissed it three times, an incident that was reported in the newspapers and taken by Thérèse as proof that her mission had been confirmed:

> I had obtained "the sign" that I had asked for, and that sign was the faithful reproduction of the graces that Jesus had granted in order to draw me to pray for sinners. Wasn't it when I was facing *Jesus' wounds*, seeing his Divine *blood* flow, that the thirst for souls had entered into my heart? I wanted to give them to drink this *immaculate blood* that must cleanse them from their stains, and the lips of "my *first child*" were pressed upon the sacred wounds!!! . . . What an expressibly sweet reply! [*SS*, p. 106]

Sweet for Thérèse, however, meant something very different than it does to most of the rest of us. To her, *sweet* didn't mean basking in ease or consolation or fun: *sweet* meant literally laying down her life. To illustrate, of the period just before she entered the convent, her sister Céline observed:

> [S]he toyed with the idea of joining a congregation of missionary sisters, but the hope of saving more souls through mortification and self-sacrifice made her decide to shut herself up in Carmel. . . . She told me the reason for this decision herself: it was in order to suffer more, and in that way win more souls for Jesus. . . . So it was this living death, which was more lucrative in souls won, that she decided to embrace, wishing, as she said herself, to become a prisoner as soon as possible, in order to bring people the beauties of heaven.

When Thérèse entered Carmel, then, she entered into solidarity with all prisoners by becoming one herself. She entered into solidarity with pregnant twelve-year-olds by abandoning herself to the self-renunciating love that all twelve-year-olds and all newborn babies crave; with suicide bombers by giving her own life but without also taking the lives of others; with outcasts and misfits the world over by embarking on a way of life whereby she resolved to voluntarily take on the hardest tasks, engage with the most difficult personalities, and treat everyone—from the most powerful to the weakest—with dignity, charity, and respect.

January 9, 1889, marked Thérèse's reception of the habit, also known as "the clothing." On September 8, 1890, she made her Profession, binding herself forever with the vows of poverty, chastity, and obedience. And on September 24, 1890, two years after entering Carmel, she took the veil, wrote her own wedding invitation, and fulfilled her lifelong dream of becoming the bride of Christ.

Just as with her prayer for Pranzini, chastity for Thérèse was no sugary adolescent dream, but a carefully considered choice encompassing far more than sexuality. Chastity includes courtesy, patience, and the refusal to force. Chastity means respecting the inner timetables, desires, weaknesses, and needs of both ourselves and others. Whether we're male or female, whatever our station in life may be, chastity protects and nourishes all that is most precious and inviolate in us, and all that is most precious and inviolate in the other.

As spiritual writer Ron Rolheiser puts it: "For Thérèse, chastity meant two, interpenetrating, things: reverence and the capacity and willingness to carry unresolved tension."

If we care about the poor and the oppressed, about abused children and rape victims, about pedophile priests and rapists, about our own broken selves, family, and friends, then being responsible with respect to our sexuality and emotions is one major way to help. That's why Thérèse took a vow of chastity. That's why she was willing to forego the warmth, reciprocity, security, and potential fulfillment of marriage in favor of what, to her, was a greater love. That's why she would later write the Apostles' Creed in blood and wear it against her heart.

Like any thinking person, Thérèse felt the inferior position of women: "Oh! Poor women, how they are disparaged! . . . It's no doubt for that reason that He allows scorn to be their lot on earth, since He chose that for Himself. . . . In heaven He'll know how to show that His thoughts are not man's thoughts (Isa. 55:8–9), because then the *last shall be first* (Matt. 20:16)" [*SS*, p. 159].

She was also well aware of the fallibility of priests: "For a month [during her Papal visit] I lived with many *holy priests,* and I saw that if their sublime dignity raises them above the angels, they are nonetheless weak and fragile men" [*SS*, p. 134].

Her solution, however, was not to lobby for rights. Her solution was not to insist that she could have done a better job, though that may well have been the case. Her solution was to make praying for priests part of her vocation—*even though she longed to be a priest herself.*

This is part of what Father Rolheiser means, if I'm interpreting him correctly, by "carrying unresolved tension." We don't pray for peace, and then treat everyone around us badly. We don't say a novena or two for the victims of abortion and rape, human trafficking, child prostitution, and sex addiction, then wring our hands. We *change our whole lives.* We do a deep and ongoing examination of conscience looking at our own sexual behavior, orientation of heart, emotional wounds. We look at the way we use other people as objects. We look at the way we are willing to take the shortcut, sexually and otherwise.

For to love means to want the spiritual well-being of the other, and that means we're called to give way, *way* more than our political views. We're called, with the help of trusted mentors, to root out the old ideas, compulsions, and patterns that drive us. We're called to be faithful to our vocations, even if nobody else seems remotely interested in our work, thoughts, sacrifices, lives. It's difficult to feel marginalized and unrecognized, but what's really hard, as you're feeling unrecognized, is to recognize and support someone else. It's difficult to minister to the poor, the hungry, the drug-, alcohol-, and sex-addicted, but what's really transformative is to get sober yourself.

Like Thérèse, I'd never much been able to reduce the mystical to the political. As appalled as I could sometimes be by the behavior of certain priests, I was deeply moved by the fidelity and sacrifice of so many others. As saddened as I could be by the Church's failure to have ever fully lived out the message of the Gospels, I loved her as my Mother. As horrified as I was by the ways that women the world over continue to be undervalued, discriminated against, marginalized, and in many cases mutilated and murdered, I also believed that I had contributed to the situation. In fact, some of my deepest wounds remained the three abortions I'd had, more than twenty years before: a form of violence, I realized now, against myself, my unborn children, the men who had fathered them; against all women, all men, all life, all hope.

My unrequited love, I realized now, was connected to that wound, sprang at least in part from a driving procreative urge that had never found its focus. That wound had assured that I felt with terrible clarity the depths of my loneliness, for I had not been with a man now in many years. Yet, precisely *because* of its depth, I began to see the value of such loneliness. I began to see that to ache for tenderness myself was to ache for the world. I began to see that in my loneliness, I entered into the loneliness of Christ. I began to see that to hold the tension of my longing, frustration, and fear was to help hold the tension of a husband who wanted to cheat on his wife; a college student who was contemplating making a quick buck by working at a strip club; a teenager, in despair over a crush gone wrong, who wanted to pull the trigger.

At daily Mass I often had a sense of how dear we women— our fidelity, our capacity to endure—must be to Christ. He sees the plodding, steady devotion of the women who come to church all over the world week in, week out; who prepare the altar, who say the Rosary, who pray the novenas, who grip the holy cards, who wear the scapulars, who carry the flame; who wait, and who, in a very real way, have kept the Church going.

They have kept the Church going—without revolt, without complaint—for the sometimes wayward priests who minister to them. They have kept the Church going while more "liberated" folk tell them they are mindless serfs who should rise up and throw off their chains. They have kept the Church going so that converts such as me can stumble in, like the five-o'clock workers in the parable of the vineyard (Matt. 20:1–16), and be "saved." They have kept the Church going so that the Church could produce—as only the Church could have produced—Dorothy Day and Blessed Teresa of Calcutta and St. Thérèse of Lisieux, as well as Archbishop Óscar

Romero and César Chávez, and St. Maximilian Kolbe. When St. Paul observed, "There is no limit to love's forbearance, to its trust, its hope, its power to endure" (1 Cor. 13:7), he must surely have been thinking of women.

"I choose all!" said Thérèse, and the further I progressed, the more I saw that the human dilemma *is* to want it all. I wanted to be a celibate, and I wanted to wantonly give myself to a spouse. I wanted the dark secrets, noise, lights, mania, and stimulation of the city, and I wanted to plant a garden, tend animals, and live on a farm. I wanted to live in the same place all my life, and I wanted to travel every inch of the globe before I died. I wanted to sit utterly still, and I was also driven to be constantly on the move. I wanted to be hidden and anonymous, and I wanted to be famous. I wanted to be close to my family, and I wanted to leave my family behind. I wanted to devote my life to activism, and I wanted to devote my life to contemplation.

I wanted to give everything to God, and I didn't know how! I longed to give my undivided self, and I couldn't! If you want all, there is only one place big enough to contain, embrace, and channel that desire, Thérèse seemed to be saying, and that is the Sacred Heart of Christ.

PRAYER

Lord, help me to offer everything of myself. All the contradictions: the part that wants to be free and the part that is afraid to be free, the part that wants to forgive and the part that won't forgive, the part that wants to let go and the part that holds on for dear life, the lion and the lamb. I can't resolve any of those warring parts myself and I have no idea what resolution would even look like.

Maybe the question isn't so much "When will I see Your face?" Maybe the question is "When will I sit still long enough to see that Your Face is everywhere?": in the quince tree outside my bedroom window, in the sparrow on the telephone wire, in the sun that, by rising every morning, and setting every night, helps me to hold the unresolved tension and encourages me to trust.

THE CONVENT

(On Shedding Our Illusions)

As for the *illusions*, God gave me the grace *not to have* ANY as I entered Carmel. I found the religious life to be as I conceived it.

—*The Story of a Soul* [p. 169]

NOT TO PUT TOO FINE A POINT ON IT, but the cloister was brimming with neurotics and misfits. Sister Mary Magdalene, who joined the Carmel several years after Thérèse, observed:

I found the community in a very disappointing state. I used to think all Carmelite nuns were saints, but I gradually became aware that at the time there were a lot of very imperfect nuns. They were noticeably lacking in silence, regularity, and especially mutual charity, and there were some lamentable divisions among them.

Chief among the neurotics was the Superior, the formidable Mother Marie de Gonzague. (For full details on life in the convent, again see Ida Görres's insightful, deliciously gossipy biography, *The Hidden Face: A Study of St. Thérèse of Lisieux*.) Some commentators have accused Mother Gonzague of almost pathological hatred, jealousy, and persecution of Thérèse:

Thérèse herself observed simply that "Our Superior [Mother Marie de Gonzague], who was often ill, had little time to be busy with me. I know that she loved me a great deal and said the best things possible about me, but nonetheless God permitted that, *without her knowing it,* she was VERY STRICT" [*SS*, p. 170].

That's one way of describing the situation. Another— opinions differ widely—would be that Mother de Gonzague was neither sufficiently astute, sensitive, nor spiritually advanced to understand Thérèse's struggles. Thérèse managed to be obedient and unflaggingly helpful nonetheless. She obeyed every order of Mother de Gonzague's, no matter how seemingly whimsical or arbitrary, to the letter. She had a phobia of spiders, but took up her cloth, as directed, and dusted under the stairwell and eaves anyway. She hand-washed the handkerchiefs of Mother de Gonzague's hoity-toity relatives who, against the general order of the chapter, were constantly visiting, chattering, gossiping, and, along with Mother's pampered cat, appropriating the nuns' community room.

Thérèse worked variously in the laundry and the sacristy; she wrote pious plays and poems for the Sisters; she was put in charge for a time of distributing the bread, water, and beer. Unaccustomed to housework of any kind—she'd hardly known how to fix her own hair or to make a bed before entering the convent—Thérèse was never particularly adept at sweeping, needlework, or any of her assigned chores. She bore the attendant reprimands and criticisms without comment, cultivated her inner life in silence, and made constant efforts to be helpful and kind to the more troublesome members of the community.

Mother de Gonzague was prioress for five long, difficult, years after Thérèse entered the convent. Even so, Thérèse was forever after grateful to her, realizing that the prioress's chief concern was not to win Thérèse's affection, but to lead her toward God:

> Oh, Mother, from how many worries does one free oneself by making the vow of obedience! How happy are simple nuns. Their only compass being the will of their Superiors, they are always assured of being on the right path. They have no fear about being wrong, even if it seems certain to them that their superiors are wrong. But when one stops looking at the infallible compass, when, under the pretext of doing God's will, one steps away from the path that she says to follow and maintains that He isn't perfectly enlightening those who nonetheless stand in His place, immediately the soul goes astray into arid paths where it is soon lacking the water of grace. Beloved Mother, you are the compass that Jesus gave me to lead me surely to the everlasting shore. [*SS*, p. 245]

The reason for obedience—from the Latin *obaedire*: to listen carefully—isn't to cede responsibility for our spiritual development, but to free ourselves for maximum devotion to that precise pursuit. For Thérèse, obedience meant learning to leave off in the middle of a word when she was writing and the prayer bell rang; to refrain from arguing back when wrongly accused; and to take the Eucharist only when allowed pursuant to convent rules, though she longed for daily communication.

Such practices might seem rigid, but to my mind they didn't seem nearly as rigid as the bondage I'd lived in for many years when I'd been obedient to nothing and no one higher than myself. Obedience in my own life had come to mean restraint of tongue and pen (admittedly practiced with extreme imperfection), the development of a writing schedule, and a daily routine that included prayer, exercise, and such simple practices as making my bed, keeping my living quarters reasonably tidy, and timely responding to phone calls, letters, and e-mails.

Such practices, however simple, tend to translate in a startlingly direct way to better relationships with those around us. They certainly worked for Thérèse. For in time, Mother de Gonzague would come to admire and cherish her, writing:

> Tall and strong, with the air of a child, with a tone of voice and an expression that hide in her the wisdom, perfection, and perspicacity of a fifty-year-old . . . a little "untouchable saint," to whom you would give the Good God without confession, but whose cap is full of mischief to play on whomever she wants. A mystic, a comic, she is everything. She can make you weep with devotion and just as easily faint with laughing during recreation.

Thérèse had no illusions about the convent, but what kind of illusions might we have? That marriage was going to be fun, that we'd adore our children every second, that a new job would save us, that he'd never look at another woman? Some of my own included that I wouldn't get cancer, wouldn't be single, wouldn't be scrambling for money at forty and fifty and closing in on sixty.

Christ never lied, but he also never promised us health, wealth, happiness, or success. That the rain falls on the just and the unjust, in fact, is one of the clearest signs of an all-intelligent Creator. It has to be that we live in a world where at any given second we can die or die out, that "bad things happen to good people": first, because we are not nearly as good as we think we are, and second, because otherwise life would be monstrous. Otherwise the universe would play favorites. We'd be rewarded for trying to walk the spiritual path. Life would be an anecdote—not an event, not a drama, not an opportunity for ongoing, ever-unfolding transformation. Otherwise, we'd spiritually die of boredom and lack of purpose. Only a world in which we're *not* rewarded, in an earthly sense, could so sublimely call us higher.

In December of 1890, influenza broke out in Carmel. Thérèse and two others were the only nuns "left standing." "Death was the rule everywhere. The sickest ones were cared for by those who could hardly walk." "I'll never be able to tell all that I saw," Thérèse observed of that ghastly period, "what life and everything that passes by seemed like to me" [*SS*, pp. 192–93].

I myself tend to have very little patience with people who are sick—partly because I've had the good luck to have seldom been sick myself; partly because I tend to think my job is to fix the sick person, and I'm afraid I don't know how to; and partly because I "learned" not to be sick when I was young: I was taught that to ask for help was a mark of poor character. So while I'm capable of deep compassion, I'm also capable, whether the person's illness is physical, emotional, or spiritual, of being like the disapproving older brother in the parable of the prodigal son (Lk. 15:11–32), silently fuming from the sidelines: "I soldiered through, now *why don't you?*"

Thus the saint distinguishes herself from the rest of us: when the epidemic had run its course, Thérèse secretly wished she were head infirmarian, so that she could take care of sick people *all the time*. Thérèse practiced charity by walking the middle way of Christ: that is, without taking up an adversarial position on the one hand, or becoming a doormat on the other. That's only possible by thinking of the "patient" as an equal, not as someone to be vanquished or subdued.

> Now I understand that perfect charity consists in bearing with others' faults, in not being surprised at their weakness, in being edified by the little acts of virtue that we see them practice. . . . [*SS*, p. 247]

> When you are exasperated with someone, the way to recover your peace of mind is to pray for that person and

ask God to reward her for giving you an opportunity to
suffer.

For the maximally difficult personality, Thérèse had Sister
Marie of St. Joseph, a neurasthenic fellow nun whom she
contrived to help in the linen room, and who had such a
polarizing, volatile temperament that she was eventually
booted out of the convent. I had my friend Fred.

Fred and I were both sober alcoholics—we'd met fifteen
years before when he was still drinking—but in other ways
we were the unlikeliest of friends. I had a law degree; Fred
was a former bronco rider. I lived to write; Fred had no use
for what he referred to as "the artsy-fartsy crowd." In his
better moments Fred was kind, generous, and appreciative,
but given his abusive childhood, his tour in 'Nam, his
decade on the streets, and the fact that over the years he'd
suffered a series of crippling and increasingly serious medical
crises—emphysema, Hepatitis C, intransigent infections on
both lungs—he could also be just a bit of a loose cannon.
He'd turn on me for no good reason. He'd give me the silent
treatment.

In the time I'd known him, I'd showed up in spite of myself
and often against my better judgment. I'd invited Fred over
for holidays. I'd sat by his hospital bed, as he lay unconscious,
and prayed. Each new crisis, I'd think, *This has GOT to be it*,
but again and again, he'd resurrected. Over the years, he'd
gone from occasional visits to the Hollywood Presbyterian
Emergency Room, to frequent stays in whatever ICU would

take him, to the board-and-care section of the VA Hospital in West Los Angeles where I'd been driving over to visit him for the last several months.

Fred had more than a touch of obsessive-compulsive disorder, which his current situation only exacerbated. "Come sit beside me, sweetie," he'd say, patting the bed, and a minute later, edgily, "Ya mind moving your leg, pal?" "Bring me a bag of M&M's next time ya come, couldja," he'd ask, "just the regular kind, no peanuts." But the kicker had been the incident a few weeks before when he'd asked for two Kit-Kats and—selfish, thoughtless, oaf that I am—I'd purchased an eight-pak, drove across town on a sweltering Saturday afternoon, and delivered those instead. "I said two, not eight," he groused, pawing the bag. "That's so alcoholic! If one's good, five is better."

"Good to see you, too," I told him, and left.

That is it, I thought. *I need to learn how to "make a boundary." I need to get rid of the dead wood in my life.* So the next day I fired off a little note. "Where were you when I had cancer?" I ranted. When have you ever given me a ride? I've done a thousand things for you and in all the years we've known each other, you've done about two for me"—which was not *strictly* true but I was mad.

There, I thought, *I've finally washed my hands of that conniving ingrate*.

I expected him to retaliate. I anticipated that our little "friendship" would come to a screeching and welcome halt. Instead, a few days later he called. "I'm sorry you feel that way," he said. "I hope we get a chance to talk soon."

That was when I saw that a guy who'd done major orphanage time as a kid, who'd taken it upon himself to help the one patient on the ward who was sicker than he was—who was dying—had finessed me on every front. That was when I saw that if I wanted to "be there" for Fred, he didn't owe me a thing, not even a thank you.

I mention Fred because one of *my* biggest illusions was that other people were meant to assuage my anxiety by filling some lack that I was responsible for filling myself. If I wanted to give, the giving had to be "for fun and for free." The giving couldn't be out of guilt, nor because I secretly wanted to get something back, nor because I wanted the other person to respond in such a way as to satisfy my longing to be useful.

Thérèse applied this same principle when Mother Marie de Gonzague appointed her assistant spiritual director of the novices at Carmel. Supremely concerned with the spiritual well-being of her charges, she was also supremely unconcerned with whether or not they liked her. She was consistently available, consistently responsive, consistently attentive, consistently engaged, and consistently detached from their reactions. She wasn't angling to be their friend, and she deflected all attempts for them to become hers. There was no untoward emotion, no drama—just the unvarnished, bracing truth.

I'd been lucky enough to have latched on to such a spiritual director myself, a woman who had also been deeply affected by alcoholism, and the experience was proving transformative. Over the course of the previous few years, she'd helped me to see that sometimes I said yes to people because I really wanted to, out of a healthy sense of charity. But sometimes I said yes because I thought the person wouldn't be able to carry on without me. Sometimes I said yes because I was afraid the person wouldn't be able to handle the disappointment. Sometimes I said yes because I thought the person wouldn't like me if I said no (interestingly, the person was often someone I didn't much like myself).

So I was learning to say no when I meant no and yes when I meant yes, as Christ had advised (Matt. 5:37). I was learning that I was never the person of last resort. I was learning to quit basing my life on questions such as: *If I take care of you, will you take care of me? If I'm "good," will I not be abandoned?*

The same approach—neither an adversary nor a doormat— holds true for disagreeable situations as for disagreeable people. I'm reminded of the night my friend Tensie's husband had a massive heart attack. Their two kids, eight and nine, were at home with Tensie's mother. Tensie, at Dennis's side in the hospital, knew he might not make it. He'd gone three full minutes without breathing. He was packed in ice.

She didn't wring her hands and hope for the best. She didn't grab the ER surgeon's arm and say, *If he dies, I'll kill you.*

She asked, "What would you do if that were your brother?

"I'd do everything I could to save his life," the doctor replied.

"Well then, do that," Tensie said. "I beg you. Because he *is* your brother."

PRAYER

Lord, relieve me of my illusions: that love is easy, that the spiritual path isn't strewn with sharp rocks. Help me to see that maybe my anger is at myself: anger at a lifetime of doing things I think are going to make other people happy. Help me instead to figure out the things that make me happy, and to do them.

True freedom—from what people think, from failure, from the fear that I'm unworthy or incapable of love—is a long way off. So I will just continue to offer up my nothingness, along with St. Thérèse, and to seek your will.

— JULY —

THE LITTLE WAY

(On the Martyrdom of Everyday Life)

But I want to seek the means of going to heaven by a little way that is very straight, very short, a completely new little way.

—*The Story of a Soul* [p. 230]

Her "little way" consisted in boasting of her infirmities, of her utter inability to do anything good.

—From the testimony of Geneviève of Saint Teresa (Thérèse's sister Céline)

When I say mortified, this is not to make you believe that I was always doing penances. Alas! I *never did a single one.* . . . My mortifications consisted in breaking my will, which was always ready to impose itself; in holding my tongue instead of answering back; in doing little things for others without hoping to get anything in return; in not slumping back when I was sitting down; etc., etc.

—*The Story of a Soul* [p. 164]

THOUGH THÉRÈSE FOUND LIFE IN THE CONVENT exactly as she expected, she suffered so greatly from the cold (the community room alone was heated; the bedrooms, chapel, refectory, and laundry room were all, in winter, frigid) that at times she actually thought she might die. The people in the kitchen, knowing she wouldn't complain, often served her the most unappetizing leftovers, re-heated multiple times. The one hour of recreation allotted to the nuns—who rose at 4 AM, gathered up to six times in the chapel, and worked the rest of the day—was given over by Thérèse to spiritually directing her novitiates or shoring up her comrades. On Thérèse's deathbed, Mother de Gonzague would deny Thérèse the morphine recommended by the doctors (to Mother's credit, on her own deathbed from cancer, she would later deny herself morphine).

It may be worth remembering as well, however, that Thérèse was taken care of financially from the moment of her birth to the moment of her death. She was surrounded, also from birth to death, by a tenderly caring family. The Carmel might have been cold in winter but the grounds were elegant, with buildings of old stone, a garden, courtyards, a fountain, and an allée of chestnut trees. As a novice Thérèse might have been given the leavings at dinner, but she never had to worry about starving. She never had to get up every morning, as millions of more "ordinary" people do, and go to a job she hated. She never had to sleep with a man she'd come to loathe and fear, as so many women do in order to protect their children. She never had to make her way in the world, as so many do today, utterly, painfully, alone.

Thérèse understood that suffering would draw her closer to Christ, in other words, but she didn't look for extra suffering; she took advantage of what came, given her living situation and station in life. She refrained from forming close emotional bonds in the convent, including with her own sisters (one of whom, Pauline, was for a time her prioress). She resisted popularity. A novice in her charge remembered once going on and on about some petty incident, to which Thérèse replied, "We're wasting our time, let's go." She knew that giving alms doesn't refer only to money, and that fasting doesn't refer only to food. We can fast from the desire to get people to like us. We can give alms by accepting whatever is offered—or not offered—in the way of warmth, encouragement, and love with thanks and praise.

This "little way" thus consists not so much in "small," hidden acts, as in offering up our entire lives, small though they may be, to the hidden suffering of Christ. Or, as Joseph F. Schmidt, FSC, puts it in another gem of a book about Thérèse, *Everything is Grace*:

> [The "little way"] was a matter of allowing the divine will to unfold in the very ordinary, everyday experiences of life and of responding with generosity, confidence, and love. In this way God would stoop down and lift her to that degree of perfection that her Beloved had prepared for her.

Still, we are saved by the small, unseen acts of others. "How often I have thought that perhaps I owe all the graces I have received to some little soul who has prayed God to give them to me, and whom I shall not meet until I reach Heaven."

And some of the best-known anecdotes about Thérèse concern her saintlike, though seemingly small efforts with respect to her fellow nuns:

1. She overcame her instinctive dislike of a particular nun, and was able to exhibit such charity, that the sister actually thought Thérèse felt a special fondness for her.

2. She stifled her almost compulsive desire to turn around and glare at the nun behind her in choir who made a clicking noise (apparently by tapping her rosary against her teeth), realizing that the more charitable act would be to pretend that the sound was music to Christ's ears and endure the annoyance in silence.

3. Every evening at dinnertime Thérèse took it upon herself to usher a particularly vexatious elderly nun from chapel to her place at table in the refectory, even going the extra mile to lovingly cut the crabapple's bread.

Saints do not live in some other world, these anecdotes tell us. They live in the same world we do, and they show us that spirituality is intensely down-to-earth. We learn to love through frustration, disappointment, and failure. We learn through the seemingly trivial incidents of our daily lives.

"When I can feel nothing, when I am altogether arid, I seek tiny occasions, real trivialities, to give joy to my Jesus: a smile, for example, or a friendly word, when I would rather be silent, or look bored," Thérèse observed, and "I prefer the monotony of obscure sacrifice to all ecstasies."

I began to see the almost superhuman strength required to refrain from, say, repeating a juicy bit of gossip, or rolling my eyes, or allowing my voice to get harsh when I was upset. I began to sense as well that, just *because* they're so difficult, such acts perhaps do far more good than we can ever know. Standing patiently in line helped the other people in line to be patient as well. Blessing the other person in traffic, even though nobody heard or saw, somehow encouraged someone else to bless the next person. When the neighborhood noise bothered me, I sometimes took to starting with one corner of my apartment complex, visualizing the person or people who lived there, and working my way around, praying for the inhabitants of each. (Other times I took to tearing out my hair and cursing.)

One observation of Thérèse's I found particularly astute was that when someone asks to borrow something that we know he or she isn't planning to give back, the impulse is to simply give the item to the person. We want to spare ourselves their paltry lies and to minimize further interaction. True charity, however, consists in lending without expectation of return, but with the happy hope that, *for the sake of the borrower*, he or she will make good the promise. True charity resists the urge to distance ourselves, in other words; to get the person off our backs.

I was reminded of contemplative theologian Richard Rohr's theory that the opposite of holding on isn't, as we tend to think, letting go—but rather participating in something greater than ourselves. Solitude, paradoxically, I was coming to see can be its own form of participation; and life in noisy, crowded Koreatown, also paradoxically, was serving as its own kind of cloister.

The Jerusalem Community, a monastic fraternity situated in the heart of various cities, notes in its *Rule of Life*:

> The city is the place of human pride, noise, idolatry, sin, massacre, and distress. . . . In the city you will have to struggle and contemplate. What the early monks set out to seek yesterday in the desert, you will find today in the city. All monastic life is a fight and urban monasticism calls for fighters. Jesus came to bring not peace but the sword. Oppose eroticism, prestige, and money, with the firm contrast of a life of poverty, humility, and purity. Fight noise with your silence; weariness with your peace; endless comings and goings with your repose in God. No cloister will protect your prayer; the countryside will not bring you serenity; the walls of your enclosure will not preserve your virtue. Followers of Christ, the Beatitudes summon you to a life of real struggle in the heart of the city.

I began to see that my little existence had a kind of strange, if virtually invisible, value; that, all along, the solitude in which I largely lived had been forming me. Walking among strangers—for Koreatown was not glittery, not hip, and way not white—had given me the freedom to find my own way. Years of praying the Divine Office every morning, of showing up at my desk, of taking a walk every afternoon, of driving in rush hour traffic to jails and psych wards to speak to fellow alcoholics, had registered. The self-styled pilgrimage I'd taken a couple of years before—when in desperation over my inability to think, pray, or act my way out of my "dark night of the soul," I'd gotten in my '96 Celica and driven cross-country and back by myself, going to Mass every day—had, all evidence seemingly to the contrary, moved me imperceptibly forward.

All around me, people were saying, "I'm spiritual, but I'm not religious. Oh no, I'm definitely not *religious.*" I wanted to reply, "Does blood not beat in your veins? Have you never ached with sorrow at the suffering of the world? Have you never cried at the flight of a bird? Have you never *fallen in love?*"

In *Owning Your Own Shadow*, Jungian analyst Robert A. Johnson notes:

> It comes as no great surprise to discover that the most powerful and valuable projection one ever makes is falling in love. This too is a shadow projection and probably the most profound religious experience one is ever likely to have. . . .To fall in love is to project the most noble and infinitely valuable part of one's being onto another human being. . . . To make this examination more difficult, we have to say that the divinity we see in others is truly there, but we don't have the right to see it until we have taken away our own projections. . . . Making this fine distinction is the most delicate and difficult task in life.

Religion isn't something we tack on to life like a crumbling doily, in other words: religion suffuses life, drives life, sets life on fire. "I came to cast fire upon the earth; and would that it were already kindled!" said Christ (Lk. 12:49). "Religion consists of the belief that everything that happens to us is extraordinarily important. It can never disappear from the world for this reason," noted the Italian poet (and suicide) Cesare Pavese. "The whole way along the human religious itinerary," observed Father Luigi Giussani, "the word *God* or *Lord*, represents the one object of man's ultimate desire, the desire to know the origin and ultimate meaning of existence."

God is a question, then: God is our deepest human desire. And it's a question that can never be fully answered, and a desire that can never be fully satisfied: the question and the desire to which Thérèse devoted her life, and around which she developed her "little way."

"[S]he rejected all ascetic efforts which were directed not toward God but toward one's own perfection." The distinction is crucial. We can try, at great personal sacrifice, to be perfectly righteous, a perfect friend, perfectly responsive, perfectly available, perfectly forgiving. But at the heart of our efforts must lie the knowledge that, by ourselves, we can do, heal, or correct nothing. The point is not to be perfect, but to "perfectly" leave Christ to do, heal, and correct in us what he wills.

A passage by Victorian poet and critic Coventry Patmore seemed beautifully to describe both Thérèse and the sort of person who might similarly be formed by following her "little way":

> There is nothing outwardly to distinguish a Saint from common persons. . . . The saint has no "fads" and you

may live in the same house with him and never find out
that he is not a sinner like yourself, unless you rely on
negative proofs, or obtrude lax ideas upon him and so
provoke him to silence. He may impress you, indeed, by
his harmlessness and imperturbable good temper, and
probably by some lack of appreciation of modern humor,
and ignorance of some things which men are expected to
know, and by never seeming to have much use for his time
when it can be of any service to you; but, on the whole, he
will give you an agreeable impression of general inferiority to yourself. You must not, however, presume upon this
inferiority so far as to offer him any affront, for he will
be sure to answer you with some quiet and unexpected
remark, showing a presence of mind—arising, I suppose,
from the presence of God—which will make you feel that
you have struck rock and only shaken your own shoulder.
If you compel him to speak about religion, . . . he will
mostly likely dwell with reiteration on commonplaces
with which you were perfectly well acquainted before
you were twelve years old; but you must make allowance
for him, and remember that the knowledge which is to
you a surface with no depth is to him a solid . . . I have
known two or three such persons, and I declare that, but
for the peculiar line of psychological research to which I
am addicted, and hints from others in some degree akin
to these men, I should never have guessed that they were
any wiser or better than myself, or any other ordinary
man of the world with a prudent regard for the common

proprieties. I once asked a person, more learned than I am in such matters, to tell me what was the real difference. The reply was that the saint does everything that any other decent person does, only somewhat better and with a totally different motive.

Just as Thérèse did from her cloister, as I went about my day I could do everything that any other decent person would but with a Christ-centered motive. I could be polite to my impolite neighbor not because he deserved politeness, but because courtesy was my policy. I could bring my sick friend cold medicine not to get good spiritual marks, but because I loved her.

I could say yes, joyfully, because the yes would allow me reciprocally to participate in the flow of the world's give and take. I could say yes because yes, whenever possible, was my stance. I could praise the amber-gold bougainvillea, the purple heliotrope, the trees laden with Meyer lemons that I passed on my walk each day. I could contribute my praise, my prayer, my silence, my stories to the world, knowing that to contribute with love always bears fruit.

One night on the 5 freeway, stuck in rush-hour gridlock, I realized that my joy, for the moment, was complete. Instead of fuming, I put on Glenn Gould—Bach's "Goldberg Variations"—and relaxed. Instead of ranting, I thought, *How splendid that I get to be part of the Mystical Body of Christ.* I looked out the window at the billboards for strip joints, the Citadel Mall with its fake Assyrian castle façade, the red neon cross on top of a church in the distance, and thought: *Only God could have imagined L.A.*

St. Augustine uses the phrase: "I happened upon myself." In the course of the journey, we happen upon ourselves.

Thérèse, I feel sure, would have agreed.

PRAYER

Lord, help me to lie fallow every so often and reassess what or whom I'm working for.

Help me to enjoy the quiet morning and the still-point of evening; the light of the moon and the incessant, slow but steady movement of the universe that fills me with love.

Help me to accept myself the way I am, not giving up the idea of healing and growth, but giving up the idea that I am ever going to reach some future point where I can rest. I can rest here.

ARIDITY

(On Praying Without Ceasing)

Dryness was my daily bread.

—*The Story of a Soul* [p. 178]

Do not think that I am swimming in consolations. Oh, no! My consolation is in not having any consolations on earth. —*The Story of a Soul* [p. 208]

She had perhaps expected to find in Carmel, the love, the raptures, the turmoil of emotions she tried to express in her poems; but God seldom discovers to us the shape of the sacrifices to come. Instead of finding consolation in her devotions, she felt nothing and had nothing to say except to offer to God this very emptiness of mind. . . . She prayed no less, but went through her prayers without the satisfaction of love felt and returned. In 1889 her "suffering" reached its height. Her spiritual aridity increased and she found no comfort in heaven or on earth. Her prayers, her Communions, lacked that sense of reality which would have made for happiness. She felt as one would, who, working and sacrificing oneself for the Beloved, received no sign that it has been noticed or appreciated; as one who would love and never hear a loving word in return.

—ÉTIENNE ROBO

THÉRÈSE'S APPROACH TO PRAYER WAS SIMPLE. Talk to God directly, she seemed to be saying. He's interested in you. He loves you like a father. Tell him your troubles, ask him for what you want, and above all, try not to overthink:

> I don't have the courage to make a strict rule for myself to search in books for *beautiful* prayers. That gives me a headache, there are so many of them! . . . And then some are more *beautiful* than others. . . . I wouldn't know how to recite them all. Not knowing which one to choose, I do as children do who don't know how to read: I very simply tell God what I want to tell Him, without making beautiful phrases, and He always understands me. [SS, p. 274]

The goal in prayer isn't to do anything "right," to acquire a technique, Thérèse seemed to be saying. The goal is surrender. "She believed it was wrong to be afraid of desiring too much or asking God for too much," observed Céline. "We must say to God: 'I know well that I shall never be worthy of the things I hope for—but I hold out my hands to You like a beggar child, and I know that You will more than grant my wishes *because You are so good!*'"

I myself had what I suppose could be called a somewhat deep prayer life, though I'd be at a loss as to how to describe it. Every morning (and sometimes at night) I prayed the Divine Office. I read and reflected upon that day's liturgy. I engaged, for anywhere from ten minutes to a couple of hours, in an activity that I was never quite sure whether to call prayer at all. Sometimes I'd just sit and look at the sunlight on the wall of my living room, or the top of the palm tree in front of the apartment building next door. Sometimes I'd simply listen to the birds. The best I can say is that I more or less disappeared. I disappeared, and when I re-emerged I felt closer to reality, more whole, more sure that everything would be all right in the end even though at the moment all seemed pain, chaos, and turmoil.

Jesus himself never gave any big meditation techniques. He said, "This is how you pray," and he gave us the Lord's Prayer. He didn't say you have to keep your back ramrod straight. He didn't say you had to learn to observe your breathing. Prayer was one area of my life that I instinctively and resolutely refrained from trying to make into a project, which is perhaps one reason the "guided mediations" in which I'd occasionally taken part over the years had left me fairly cold.

I much preferred Adoration—sitting before the Blessed Sacrament in prayerful silence—at, say, Immaculate Heart of Mary, a relatively poor, largely Filipino parish in East Hollywood. Here, folks would be snuffling, sneezing, hacking; some kneeling, some sitting. Sweaters hung askew off shoulders, rosaries dangled from arthritic fingers. Some eyes were closed, some were open, staring, stricken; people were doubled over, head in hands; people were crying.

This seemed to me just the atmosphere in which the Son of Man would have felt at home. I know I did. Here, I could imagine myself the "prodigal daughter" with my head buried in the Father's breast. Here I could imagine myself to be Job saying, *My God, though thou slayest me, yet will I put my trust in thee.* Here I could hear my heart crying, *Bind up my gaping, hemorrhaging wounds. Tell me what I'm to do next, Father, where I belong. Lord Jesus Christ, have mercy on me, a sinner.*

Sometimes I could also feel my whole being "speaking" Christ as I went about my routine of work, errands, exercise, socializing, Mass, occasional travel. Increasingly, I was marginally better able to handle setbacks, frustration, loneliness. A forgetful friend stood me up for lunch, and within minutes, I'd let the incident go. I noticed I didn't *always* have to have the last word. One day someone nabbed the parking space I was going to pull into and—*without swearing*—I simply drove on and found another.

Still, when I got really quiet, I could feel a heaviness with which I went to sleep and woke—a weight I could neither identify nor explain. I sometimes came to consciousness in the morning to find myself in the midst of an imaginary argument with an unseen adversary. I seemed to be subconsciously justifying or defending myself—against whom or what I wasn't sure.

I began to see that my prayer was perhaps not so subtly manipulative. I genuinely wanted to get closer to God, yet I also seemed to be maintaining a distance. I seemed to be subconsciously trying to skew things my way, thinking I needed to help God along. All my life I had had a burning hunger; a drive for meaning that, with time, had only grown. I had found my way to sobriety, writing, and the Church, but what gnawed at me was whether I was still in some way "missing the mark." I did not understand why, in spite of my hunger for relationship, one had not materialized. Neither did I understand the very deep pull to solitude I had felt since childhood. Sometimes I wondered if I was too much alone, and sometimes I wondered whether I should be alone more—whether I actually had a calling to be a contemplative hermit—which is *kind* of funny, but not really.

I don't in any way mean that I was, or wanted to be, or fancied myself, a "lone wolf." Good Lord, no. I needed people desperately. I was grateful for every moment of companionship. More to the point, the Church was my life-blood. The Church was my anchor, my heart. The Church had taken me in when no one else would have me.

The people who preached poverty so often hated the Church! "How can you go to church?" they'd ask. "How can you stand the homilies, the music, the bad architecture, the hypocrites?" And I would think: *You don't know what poverty is. You have never known the poverty of being so poor in human companionship, so starved for human contact, so hungry for the truth that you stumbled into church like a drowning man seizes a raft. You have never been poor enough that you have been so grateful for whoever turned up in the pew beside you, for a smile, for a priest who said Mass, that you have fallen to your knees and sobbed. You don't know what it is to be poor until you have no family, no man, no friend who understands your heart, no one to support your work to which, day after day, year after year, in silence, in solitude, you give your life.*

I saw how Christ had slowly, inexorably, unerringly guided me to the experiences that would lead me closer to him. I saw how the "cloister" of Koreatown had connected me to all the suffering and problems of the world while also shielding me in some sense from the temptations of the world: the "temptation to be relevant" as Henri Nouwen put it. In Koreatown, where Caucasians were a distinct minority, I was not esteemed, I was not consulted, I was in some sense forgotten, scorned, rejected, or more often simply ignored.

I saw, too, how, even though I'd been educated as a lawyer, and lived in L.A., and had friends who were in the world, I was still not exactly of the world: I never had been. I'd been a blackout drunk for twenty years, and then I'd gotten sober, and married, and divorced, and written, but even when I'd been doing "normal" things I'd known that real life lay in a realm beyond.

I did not, for instance, watch TV. I did not read about or listen to or pay any attention to politics. I didn't need to watch politics to know that we were doing terrible, terrible violence to ourselves and each other: financially, sexually, emotionally, physically, spiritually. I saw the billboards. I read the *New York Times Book Review*. I did not need to immerse myself more fully in culture; I needed to walk down the street and look at people's faces, to love them, to see their hunger. I needed to feel the suffering of the world and to see with horror how I had contributed to it. I needed to undergo not penance, not punishment, but a kind of purification.

And the Church, I saw more and more, was where purification happens in earnest. "I am the way, and the truth, and the life," Christ had said (Jn. 14:6), and what is Christ except his Church that he built on Peter—on one of us: wayward, fickle, frightened? The Church is where we learn of our true intolerance, our hatred, our impatience, our cowardice, our incessant judgments, our coldness, our hardness of heart, our complete lack of love. Church confronts us with our idol-worship of people, places, and things that are other than God. We want to choose whom we love; with whom we worship. We want to be better than other people, especially in church. Church is often the last place we want to be, and in the end, the first place we can, and must, be.

My feeling was not sentimentality, but rather a function of my belief in the Real Presence: that in the words of consecration during the Eucharistic prayer, the bread and wine become the real—not the actual, or virtual—but the real Body and Blood of Christ. To participate in the Mass of the Catholic Church is to participate in an event of unimaginable significance.

As Carl Jung observed in an essay entitled "Transformation Symbolism in the Mass":

> The ritual event that takes place in the Mass has a dual aspect, human and divine . . . Christ incarnates as a man under the aspect of the offered substances, he suffers, is killed, is laid in the sepulcher, breaks the power of the underworld, and rises again in glory. . . . What happens in the consecration is essentially a miracle, and is meant to be so, for otherwise we should have to consider whether we

were not conjuring up God by magic, or else lose ourselves in philosophical wonder how anything eternal can act at all, since action is a process in time with a beginning, a middle, and an end. It is necessary that the transubstantiation should be a cause of wonder and a miracle which man can in no wise comprehend. It is a *mysterium.* . . . What in the world could induce us to represent an absolute impossibility? What is it that for thousands of years has wrung from man the greatest spiritual effort, the loveliest works of art, the profoundest devotion, the most heroic self-sacrifice, and the most exacting service? What else but a miracle? It is a miracle which is not man's to command; for as soon as he tries to work it himself, or as soon as he philosophizes about it and tries to comprehend it intellectually, the bird is flown. A miracle is something that arouses man's wonder precisely because it seems inexplicable.

Mass was like being on the greatest stage set that had ever and ever could be produced. Mass was to participate in an ancient, ever-unfolding cosmic drama. Mass was to understand that I was participating in the kingdom of God regardless of any particular emotion I felt, thought I had, or action I performed.

Mass was to reflect on the fact that Thérèse, for all her holiness, all her sanctity, all her prayer, all her love, had experienced spiritual dryness since practically the day she entered Carmel.

In spite of my own aridity, for my own part as I went about my days I found myself ever so slightly less lonely. I found myself ever so slightly less cowed when the laudable action of another was praised in my presence. But perhaps nowhere did the fruits of prayer reveal themselves more clearly than that, through no real thought or effort of my own, I found myself attending Mass almost daily.

This came as a bit of a surprise as I'd often made efforts in that direction before, but with spotty success. How could I have time for all my other obligations? How would I get my work done?

Some days I drove, but mostly I walked the five long blocks, through traffic and honking horns, past the grand old apartment buildings, the Dong-A Book Plaza, the parking lot attendant at Heyri Coffee with whom, after many years, I was at last on nodding terms, the abandoned lot from which I sometimes plucked a frond of wild fennel through the chain link fence, and across Wilshire Boulevard to St. Basil's, built in the late 1960s, with its soaring concrete walls, high, narrow stained-glass windows and echoing sanctuary.

Here, I cast my lot with whatever other rag-tag dregs of humanity walked through the doors: the homeless Hispanic man sleeping on the pew beside me, the Korean matron, the Vietnamese nun, in her sneakers and veil. Like Thérèse, I had no one with whom to share my deepest inner life. As an alcoholic, I knew all too well my bereftness, my nothingness. To have been born in some sense mentally ill was also to have been rendered so poor in spirit as to burn with love for

Christ and his imperfect, shabby, sometimes embarrassing Church.

Many days I was so distracted or anxious that I could barely hear a single word. Other times a phrase I'd heard a thousand times would strike me with the force of revelation. Daily Mass changed the way I ordered my time. Daily Mass forced me to pause. Daily Mass made me feel simultaneously broken and triumphant, consoled and afraid. That the sacrifice upon which the world had been saved was re-enacted each day in the shadow of Tofu Cabin and Gentle Dental simultaneously mystified, moved, depressed, and cheered me.

I took in the Gospel; I listened to the homilies. I wept, I sighed, I gratefully concurred, I mentally argued. But all the while I was obeying. At a level way deeper than I could hear with my ears, I was listening carefully.

Out on Wilshire again—Golf Town, Nara Bank—I'd think: *No one knows I go to Mass; no one would care if I didn't.* Walking home, I'd think: *Was that a dream?*

But more and more, I saw that Christ was the realest thing there was.

PRAYER

Oh God, have mercy on us. Show us how to love each other.
I don't know how to love. I can't separate my pain from self-pity, dishonesty, selfishness. I don't know how to turn my will and my life over to your care.
Sometimes I can't feel you anywhere: not in solitude, not when I'm with people.

Sometimes I feel like any move I make is wrong.

Sometimes I feel as if I'm invisible and that no one sees or cares about the good I try to do.

Sometimes I feel like I'm going to be alone all my life.

Sometimes I don't trust anyone, and maybe you, dear God, least of all.

THE LONG, SLOW DECLINE OF THÉRÈSE'S FATHER

(On Being Stripped Down)

If you are willing to bear serenely the trial of being displeasing to yourself, you will be for Jesus a pleasant place of shelter. You will suffer, of course, for you will be outside the door of your own home; but have no fear, the poorer you are the more Jesus will love you.

—IDA FRIEDERIKE GÖRRES

THE CATHOLIC WORKER, CALLED BY SOME the most influential lay movement of the twentieth century, began in the Depression-era Bowery and emphasizes personalism, the works of mercy, and "voluntary poverty." Co-founder Dorothy Day's favorite saint was Thérèse. But as Day, whom I'd long admired, well knew, true poverty is never, ever voluntary. Poverty consists precisely in all the ways you absolutely *don't* want to be poor. Poverty consists in a long succession of events not going your way. Poverty consists in being stripped down to nothingness. Poverty consists in your beloved father's slowly going crazy.

Soon after Thérèse entered the convent, Louis Martin began the descent into a slow, and what would eventually transpire to be almost complete, mental deterioration. Rumors initially circulated around town that this good and pious man suffered from syphilis or, even more distressing, that his youngest daughter's entry into the convent had driven him insane.

Thérèse was devastated:

> I remember . . . at the moment of our first ordeal [when Papa disappeared for four days and turned up miles away], I said "I'm suffering a lot, but I feel that I can endure even greater trials." I wasn't thinking then about the ones that were reserved for me. . . . I didn't know that on the twelfth of February, one month after my taking the habit, our beloved father would drink the *bitterest,* the *most humiliating* of all cups [by being obliged to enter the Bon Sauveur mental hospital in Caen] . . . Oh! That day I didn't say that I would be able to suffer more!!! . . . Words can't express our anguish, so I'm not going to try to describe it. [*SS,* p. 177]

The decline continued for three years: three years of being stripped down yet further, three years during which Thérèse watched even more of the things she held dear go by the wayside: the family name; the person in the world who no doubt loved her most, and had certainly loved her longest; any hope of watching her beloved father enjoy a peaceful, dignified dotage. Those three years of growing in maturity—of enduring the continuing trials of interior dryness, the "persecution" of being misunderstood, and Mother de Gonzague's personality quirks—perhaps revealed to her in a whole new way that "the poorer you are, the more Jesus loves you."

For in spite of her anguish, Thérèse was able to write to her sister Pauline: "One day in heaven we will love to talk to each other about our *glorious* times of trial. . . . Yes, the three years of Papa's martyrdom seemed to me to be the most pleasant, the most fruitful of our entire life" [*SS*, p. 177].

Such serene acceptance, I must admit, sometimes struck me as ever-so-slightly exasperating. Why Thérèse's *insistence* on martyrdom: on turning the velvet in the sewing basket wrong side out so as to deprive herself of the smooth, pretty nap; on joy when the pretty pitcher was taken from her room and replaced with one that was old and cracked? Why contrive to make everything ugly, drab, base except to draw attention to oneself, to compete to see who can make do with the least?

But Thérèse's joy with the cracked pitcher was no superficial show of asceticism. The point is never a contest to see who can be poorest, nor who can suffer most. The point, which Thérèse honed all her life, is whether we're willing to detach from the things of the world—to be stripped down—in order to grow in love. "It would certainly be unfair to call Thérèse of Lisieux limited, narrow. She was very alert and intelligent, and could certainly have gone to university today, passing all examinations with flying colors. But her horizon was limited—she was quite definitely a vertical person, could only grow skyward and into the depths—no breadth."

One place Thérèse "grew skyward" was with a particular sister in the convent who grated dreadfully on her nerves but toward whom Thérèse was determined never to show the slightest sign of aversion. She didn't make a project out of the woman, but she went out of her way to be pleasant, kind, and helpful, to the point that the nun was once heard to remark that she didn't know what Thérèse saw in her that she had singled her out as a special friend. Part of our poverty as followers of Christ, in other words, is the poverty of making ourselves always available, of being profligate toward everybody: even as the life is almost being drained out of us, even when we would so much rather go off and mourn our own losses and griefs in private.

Christ—as always, the model—never sat back, crossed his arms, and dismissed the annoying, the troublesome, or the unpromising. He never name-called, never judged, never treated a single person with contempt. Christ talked to everybody, he mingled with everybody, he shared his message with everybody, and he also loved everybody.

So we don't count the cost with anybody, either. We don't waste our time with people who don't want what we have to offer. But if they do, one form of martyrdom is to give a listening ear or an understanding smile to all comers: the borderline-personality alcoholic who's trying to get sober; the friend with the broken heart that refuses to mend; the charismatic prayer group whose sensibility didn't remotely jibe with mine and whose offer to speak at their quarterly brunch I joyfully, gratefully accepted because we are all in our ways trying to walk toward the light. (Don't think I didn't need the $250 stipend either.)

We're called to speak to people to whom we often don't feel like speaking; to refrain from surrounding ourselves with people "just like us," whose thoughts, ideas, and actions we can more or less manage and control; to share not just with the poor, but with the rich, the mediocre, the irritating, the Republicans, the Democrats, because we never know who the poor are. We never know whose heart is hemorrhaging. We never know who needs a kind word, a smile, a helping hand.

Part of the overall plan seems to be that no matter how sad, wounded, neurotic, or needy we are, that may be exactly what some other person needs us to be at that time. We don't know the ways we comfort and save each other, not only in spite of our wounds, but also in some cases, *because* of them. No one is likely to be more sympathetic to an alcoholic than another alcoholic. No one is likely to have more compassion than the person, guided by love, who needs compassion him or herself. That is why we must never judge. That is why we must always look for the good in the other.

As if to drive the point home, right around this time a series of incidents occurred where I judged someone, only to discover later that the person had undergone some terrible trauma. *He's so angry*, I thought about one young man, then learned he'd witnessed his alcoholic mother knife his father to death. *She dresses so revealingly*, I sized up another gal, then found that she'd been raped by her uncle as a child. These people were doing way better than I would have done under similar circumstances. Each person has a cross to bear, and they were bearing theirs more patiently than I ever could. I couldn't bear theirs; I was too weak. That other person had been given his or her particular cross to bear, and was bearing it bravely.

Similarly, I began to realize that I was capable of committing any sin that anyone else had committed. In this way, even, say, pedophile priests didn't shock me quite so much. I could imagine humans so hungry for love, so enchanted by innocence or beauty or the very mystery of human flesh, that they crossed a line that should never, ever be crossed. If I squinted, I could "see" the terrorists: the lust to be right, to be avenged. I wanted to say I couldn't see the torturers, but if I thought long and hard enough, I could see the torturers. We do want to hurt people sometimes, to inflict pain.

I began to see the value of refraining from criticizing and complaining. The goal isn't to masochistically endure conditions that we could change, if we were willing to make the effort. The goal is to adopt a general policy of not complaining about things that can't be changed, not because we enjoy being rigidly ascetic but because complaining about our private sorrows—traffic, the cost of living, our health, our endless suffering—is not helpful. I began to notice how, when someone called me to "vent," I felt as if I myself needed an oxygen tank when I got off the phone. I noticed the effect people had on me when they announced, for example,

"My family is driving me crazy!" or in a woebegone tone, "Sometimes I just feel like I'm not going to make it." What could I possibly expect my friends to do when I made such statements to them?

I almost always went to Mass by myself, and I was often sort of shoved aside by big families who crawled over me or elbowed me aside and took over the pew, and then ignored me or turned away at the Sign of Peace (the portion of the Mass, just before receiving the Eucharist, when we greet those around us by a smile, a nod, a handshake, a hug, a kiss). Though understandable, this made for a certain way of being invisible, and could make me feel like the poorest of the poor, especially on Sunday, which is often a hard day for those of us who are making our way more or less alone, and for whom a simple handshake, a kind glance, a human touch, means all the difference.

And yet—more and more I saw that to partake in some small way in Christ's loneliness and poverty is part of the scandal of the Cross. My task, instead of complaining, was to pray for purity of heart, to rejoice in the families at church, to get a kick out of their kids, to welcome those around me whether or not they were able to welcome me, and then to take all that out into the world: to the lonely, the lovers, the people old enough to be my parents, the people young enough to be my children.

My task also, of course, was to continue to struggle with my massive limitations and flaws. One morning I was out on the balcony of my apartment, surrounded by my beloved succulents and bromeliads, praying to go into the world as an anonymous, hidden presence of Christ's infinite love, as much as someone so frail, fallen, and weak could be. Just then I saw, really saw, the seedling my eyes were trained on, and the leaf was a brilliant beautiful vivid green streaked along the upper part with bright red, like blood. It was almost as if God were saying: *Yes, yes, that's just it. You'll bear fruit—but you'll bleed first—as Thérèse did. You'll burst into leaf, but you'll be pruned first—as Thérèse was.*

Shortly afterward, I came across a poem by German novelist and poet Gertrud von le Fort (1876–1971), written two years before her conversion to Catholicism:

> You alone have sought my soul!
>> Who shall belittle the right of your fidelity?
> My soul was like a child
>> that has been secretly exposed and left to die.
> She was an orphan at all the banquets of life
>> and a widow in the arms of her lover.
> My brothers have despised her
>> and my sisters have treated her like a stranger.
> Those whom the world held wise have betrayed her.
> When she thirsted they told her: "All things are
>> passing!"
>> And when she was in anguish they said: "But you
>> are nothing!"
> They sent her to my heart
>> as though she were a drop of its blood.

They sent her to my intellect
    as though she were but a thought.
She was like a wild beast in a forest of dark drives
    and like a frightened bird in a dead universe.
She was like a woman who spends her life dying.
But you prayed for her and this was her salvation.
You have sacrificed for her and this has been her food.
You have mourned for her as for a lost jewel,
    and for this she shouts out your name with joy.
You have raised her up as a queen
    and for this she lies at your feet.
Who shall belittle her the right of your fidelity? . . .

When she thirsted they told her: "All things are passing!"
    And when she was in anguish they said, "But you are
        nothing!"
She was like a woman who spends her life dying. . . .

I recognized Thérèse, and at last, I recognized myself. At last someone had told my story. For the last ten years especially, I had been in anguish and "they"—my husband, the person I loved, the legal profession, the medical profession when I had cancer, the publishing industry—had said in so many words: "But you are nothing." Everywhere I had turned: a blank wall. Everything I had hoped: ashes. Everything I had worked for: "But you are nothing." For so long, my heart had silently cried: *Who am I? Where am I?* For so long, I had been in darkness, doubt, and close to despair. One morning in the shower I wept to Christ: "I don't love you and you don't love me either!"

The very next day something shifted. Von le Fort's poem had clarified, validated, corroborated something in me. That the world had said, "But you are nothing," didn't mean that I wasn't also fallen and broken and sinful; that I didn't often say to other people, in so many words, "You are nothing." But that time after time, I had said, "I am in anguish," and the world had said, "You are nothing," was not an exaggeration. I was not crazy. I was not making things up. The purpose of the clarification wasn't to allow me to wallow in self-pity: my lot was no worse, and for that matter, no better, than the next person's.

The purpose of the clarification was simply to help me understand how to proceed and where to go from here. And more and more the only explanation seemed to be that Christ, in spite of our little lover's quarrel, had chosen me. He had given me his Church, which alone had said, "You are something." His Church had seen what was precious in me and allowed it to flower. And now he wanted all of me. He wanted to strip me down to nothing. He wanted me to surrender completely.

That might sound a little high-blown—except that he chooses all of us, if we are given the grace to see and hear.

So I'd been chosen—and life went on. I'd been chosen—and I quickly forgot I'd been chosen. I'd been chosen—and the universe continued to exhibit its vast sense of humor. I called a friend hoping to weasel my way into the Gloria Swanson–type

'30s Hollywood complex where she lived, and instead the friend asked me for a ride to her doctor's. I wanted the call to be from my editor, and instead the call was from someone asking me to drive miles outside of town to a juvenile camp to talk to the kids about booze and drugs. I wanted the call to be from the man of my dreams, whoever that might be, and instead the call was from a friend asking me to be the godmother to one of his newborn twin daughters.

Perhaps being stripped down to nothingness means this: over and over again, discovering that God gives us what we need, not necessarily what we want.

PRAYER

Lord, when the world tells me I am nothing, help me to remember that you are not of the world.

When everything I do turns to ashes, help me to remember to turn to you.

When everywhere I turn is a blank wall, help me to see your face.

When I feel like an orphan, help me to remember that you are my Father.

When I feel like a frightened bird in a dead universe, help me to remember that love reigns eternal.

When I feel like I'm being stripped down to nothing, help me to know that you are especially near.

THE STORY OF
A SOUL

(On Offering Up Our Work)

Of her life in the convent there is little to say in the way
of external events. Her fights, her victories in the spiritual
order were largely hidden from the eyes of others.

—ÉTIENNE ROBO

UNTIL CLOSE TO HER DEATH, THÉRÈSE CONTINUED to be
largely unremarked by her fellow nuns. Sister Anne of the Sacred
Heart reported, of her own years at Carmel: "There was nothing
to say about her. She was very kind and very retiring, there was
nothing conspicuous about her. I would never have suspected
her sanctity." Thérèse's sister Céline observed: "She considered
it harder for human nature to work without ever seeing the fruit
of one's labors, to toil on without encouragement or any kind of
relief. She said the hardest work of all was to work on oneself in
order to gain self-mastery."

Outwardly, Thérèse's life might have been unremarkable;
inwardly, however, she burned, as she had since childhood,
with the desire to be a saint, or more specifically, a martyr.
Anyone who labors under the misapprehension that the "Little
Flower" was soft or sentimental has never read this:

Like You, my Beloved Bridegroom, I would like to be scourged and crucified. . . . I would like to die by being skinned alive like St. Bartholomew. . . . Like St. John, I would like to be plunged into boiling oil. . . . With St. Agnes and St. Cecilia, I would like to present my neck to the sword, and like Joan of Arc, my dear sister, I would like to be burned at the stake, murmuring your name, *Jesus*. [*SS*, p. 215]

Thérèse wanted to be a saint, but she never agonized for a second over how that might happen, whether or how the rest of the world might come to know, or how God might achieve the feat with such an unlikely candidate: "This desire might seem foolhardy, if one were to consider how weak and imperfect I was, and how much I still am after seven years spent in the religious life, but nonetheless I still feel the same audacious confidence [formed as a child] that I'll become a great Saint" [*SS*, pp. 70–71].

She continued to labor over her inner trials in obscurity. She concerned herself not with her own glory, but with the glory of God. Then, in the winter of 1894, Mother Pauline, at Sister Marie of the Sacred Heart's urging and almost in passing, ordered Thérèse to write the memoirs of her childhood.

As a matter of obedience and humility Thérèse complied; as a matter of obedience and humility she gave her whole heart to the effort. Any author will blanch at the conditions under which she was expected to write: in a cheap lined notebook, with constant interruptions, sitting in a chair during odd snatches of the one hour of "recreation" the nuns had each day.

Any author will blanch at the response: when Thérèse presented the finished manuscript, Pauline threw the pages into a drawer and didn't so much as glance at them for two months.

When Pauline finally did get around to the manuscript, however, she was bowled over: "I said to myself: *And this blessed child . . . is still in our midst! I can speak to her, see her, touch her. Oh! how she is unknown here. And how I am going to appreciate her more now!*"

The tree had at last begun to show its fruit. The result would come to be known as "Manuscript A," and comprise chapters 1 through 8 of *The Story of a Soul*. And the rest, as they say, is history.

Though *we* know the inner work of a lifetime would be revealed to the entire world, however, at the time, Thérèse didn't. Though *we* know that, after her death, her book would become an instant sensation, be translated into.over sixty languages, and eventually sell over one hundred million copies—she didn't. And if she never had doubts, we certainly do. We might feel stuck: in an office job we don't like, with a sick child or parent. We might be conflicted about the work we do: wondering whether we're serving God, wondering whether we're serving ourselves.

For my own part, I had always seen writing as a religious vocation. I had never been much interested in literary scenes;

I was interested in "the habit of art"; I was interested in as deep and authentic a life, ordered to writing, as possible. Certain things had gone by the wayside—my marriage, a steady income, health insurance, a social life—but I didn't think of them as sacrifices. On the contrary, that someone as weak and anxious as I was had managed to leave the relative prestige of a job as a lawyer and set out at the age of forty-one to write—with no mentor, no support, no guide other than the fixed, rock-bottom conviction that writing was my calling—was one of the surest signs I knew of a loving God.

I also knew that my passion for writing stemmed from perhaps the wrong reason: my idea that if my love would not bear fruit in a person, maybe it would bear fruit in my work. If I could not focus my love on a person, at least I could focus it on my essays and stories and books. That opened me to a different kind of pain when, as had happened of late, my work was not succeeding in the way I'd envisioned, and was one more illusion of which I recognized, however dimly, that I was being, or would have to be, stripped.

Christ, too, labored in obscurity, and we might reflect that similar long deserts, where all our efforts seem to go unrecognized, are necessary to the formation of our souls. During years of darkness when we anonymously tend our flame, we can rest assured that the flame will blaze somehow, somewhere—maybe not in our lifetimes. But like the candle passed from hand to hand in church on Christmas Eve, then carried aloft to the altar to light the Advent candle, we all do our part. Maybe we are raising children so that our children can raise children. Maybe we are unknowingly holding the world together by trying to do a good job for an employer we dislike. Maybe I would write my whole life in order that one person might come to Christ.

If so, I would do well to follow in the footsteps of Thérèse, who prefaced *The Story of a Soul* with: "[I]t isn't about my life, properly speaking, that I'm going to write, it's about my thoughts concerning the graces that God has consented to grant me" [*SS*, p. 4].

Story was of particular interest to me because in a way, my work *consisted* in telling my story. In a way, I also was coming to see, there is only one story (and an infinite number of ways to tell it): the story of death and resurrection. That was Christ's story, that was Thérèse's story, and that was very much the story of the alcoholic who gets sober.

The story can't be "I'm a victim" and it also can't be "I'm a hero," though in some sense you're telling of the hero's journey. What makes for an authentic personal story is that the hero is not you; the heroes are the people who put up with or helped you or accompanied you along the way. The star of the story is not you; the star is something greater than you. The astonishment of the story is never that the world finally recognized your genius and showered you with the love and attention you so richly deserve. The story is that a God exists who is so kind, so loving, so merciful, that he sees fit to forgive all your transgressions, wrong turns, and mistakes; a God who ministers, with infinite tenderness, to all the hurt that's been done to you and all the hurt you've done to others, and welcomes you back to the banquet table.

Just as the Gospels mostly lead up to the Passion, then give us a very short, very patchy glimpse of the Resurrection, an alcoholic's story—what it was like, what happened, what it's like now—is generally about three-quarters "drunkalogue" and one-quarter sobriety. That's not because sobriety is less "important," but because the Resurrection is inherent in the way the story is told—that is, with humility, gratitude, and often humor that would do the nearest Comedy Club proud.

When you're "in" the Resurrection, you also still bear the wounds. You haven't shut the door on the wounds, but the way you talk about the wounds changes; the wounds, and the incurring of them, become right-sized. A sober drunk doesn't minimize the agony of his or her drinking, but the point of the story is that out of that pain came a "resurrected" life ordered to service, to joy.

Similarly, Thérèse didn't minimize the impact of her mother's death, her father's descent into madness, the anguish of her aridity; she focused on the grace of God that works in spite of, and even by virtue of, our pain. The Gospels don't minimize the Crucifixion; they showcase its horror by focusing on the glory, nobility, mystery, and cataclysmically earth-shaking message of the God-Man who was nailed to the Cross. They showcase its horror by showing that in our ongoing attempts to murder Christ, we attempt to murder integrity, truth, beauty, love. They showcase the Resurrection by reporting that Christ cannot die, will never die, has vanquished death.

Just as in the Gospels, in "real life" the Resurrection is patchy, ephemeral, incapable of being held on to. Just as in the Gospel of Luke—when on the road to Emmaus the disciples recognized Christ in the breaking of bread, and he immediately vanished from their sight—an authentic story, such as Thérèse's, describes our moments of joy and our epiphanies on earth as fleeting. An authentic story imparts the sense that—just as Christ is described post-Resurrection in the Gospels—sometimes we "see" him, sometimes we don't; sometimes we recognize him in the flesh; sometimes we experience him more as spirit. That's another reason, I was beginning to see, Christ instituted a church: so that the whole broken lot of us could gather around the table, throw our talents, gifts, stories, wounds—healed and unhealed—into the pot, and together create something unexpected, strange, and new.

If the Church was revealing to me my poverty, increasingly, the Church was also revealing to me the hidden, mysterious dimension in people and things. One night, walking from 24-Hour Fitness to the Pio-Pico Library, a familiar figure arose from the shadows: Gene, the homeless guy who hung around St. Basil's; Gene, who smoked a pipe and thought the CIA had tapped into his brain; Gene, who wore a heavy down parka even on the hottest summer days, standing in the light of a street lamp.

"We've been friends for a long time," he began.

"Yes, we have, Gene," I agreed.

"I was wondering if you might have a dollar and a quarter for the bus."

My wallet was in my gym bag, so I set my books and purse on the ground and started rummaging through.

"I don't want to put you out now," Gene added. "I know you may be on a budget."

"No, that's okay, I have it." I dug out a couple of bucks, handed them over, and bent to gather up my things.

"Take your time," he offered gallantly. "I'm gonna stand right here and protect you." I straightened and we stood for a moment: two fragile, weary human beings, face to face, in the shadowy light. I suddenly realized that Gene—teeth stained brown with nicotine, reeking of B.O.—was the first person I'd talked to all day. Gene—a beggar concerned about my budget—had shown me more tenderness than any male had in a long time.

"Oh, Gene, that is so nice," I said and, turning to leave, instinctively blew him a kiss. *I kissed a leper*, I thought wonderingly all the way home. *That was like the conversion of St. Francis of Assisi when he kissed the leper.*

To see the leper in someone else is of course to get deeply in touch with the leper in yourself. *Will anyone see my writing?* I sometimes thought. *Is this the way to spend my life?* Then I'd realize that Thérèse's dryness must have made her, too, sometimes wonder whether she should have traveled about the world spreading the word of God; whether she should have been a doctor, a missionary, a social reformer; whether she'd made a mistake by cloistering herself in an undistinguished, obscure convent.

"Failure, then failure! so the world stamps us at every turn," observed William James. "A process so ubiquitous and everlasting is evidently an integral part of life." "There is indeed one element in human destiny that not blindness itself can controvert," added Robert Louis Stevenson. "Whatever else we are intended to do, we are not intended to succeed; failure is the fate allotted."

So take heart: All ye losers of the world, unite! To fail is to participate in the richness and fullness of life; to fail in the short run is the way of Christ. We don't want to fail; we don't strive to fail. But to succeed all the time would lead to a different kind of hell. To feel constant consolation would derogate the need to seek God.

When a person dies whose existence has been all comfort and ease, we might be envious of the comfort, but we also sense that he or she has missed some essential point. When someone dies who has suffered, on the other hand, we might feel compassion, or pity, or even that the person brought the suffering upon him or herself. But we also think: *Ah—that person lived.*

PRAYER

Help me to refrain from lashing out at others when I'm feeling that everything I've worked for has come to naught.

Help me to remember that Christ himself died the most ignominious of deaths, his life's work an apparent failure.

Help me to rejoice in the prosperity and success of those
  around me.
Help me not to be afraid of the leper in myself and others.
Help me to see that the only success lies in seeking Christ.
Help Gene.

MY VOCATION
IS LOVE!

(On Letting Our Flame Burn Hot)

In the seven years since she'd entered Carmel, Thérèse had abandoned herself ever more fully to God: "*Se livrer*"—this she repeated again and again, until the hour of her death: to yield, to surrender unconditionally, to abandon oneself entirely, to give oneself over entirely to another's keeping.

—IDA FRIEDERIKE GÖRRES

The great saints have worked for God's glory, but I, who am only a very little soul, I work only for His pleasure, His whims. And I would be happy to bear the greatest sufferings—even without God's knowing it, if this were possible—not for the purpose of giving Him a passing glory, but if only I knew that in this way a smile would rise to his lips.

—Thérèse, from a conversation with
her sister Marie, July 16, 1897

EVER MORE THÉRÈSE BURNED FOR CHRIST; ever more she longed to give herself at a deeper level, ever more she knew that "Jesus can't desire useless sufferings for us, and that He wouldn't inspire in me the desires that I feel if He didn't want me to fulfill them" [SS, p. 205]. She knew that "dazzling works" were beyond her reach; behind the convent walls, she could neither preach the gospel nor shed her blood— but how to "bear witness to her Love, since Love is proved by works" [SS, p. 219].

She had often pondered the possibility of offering herself as a victim of God's *justice*—a spiritual practice that was in vogue at the time and consisted in offering oneself up in place of a wrongdoer to suffer the consequences of the wrong. This rather harsh view of justice didn't appeal to her, however; and on June 9, 1895, the feast day of the Holy Trinity, kneeling behind the grille for Sunday Mass she was finally given "the grace to understand" her mission in all its fullness:

> "Oh, my God!" I cried in the depths of my heart, "will it only be Your Justice that will receive souls that offer themselves as sacrificial victims? . . . Doesn't your Merciful *Love* need them as well? . . . It seems to me that if You found souls that were offering themselves as sacrificial victims to Your Love, You would consume them rapidly. It seems to me that You would be happy not to dam up the waves of infinite tenderness that are within You. . . . If Your Justice, which extends only over the earth, likes to vent itself, how much more does your Merciful Love desire to *set souls on fire*, since your Mercy rises all the way to heaven [Ps. 36:5]. . . . Oh, my Jesus! Let *me* be that happy victim; consume your sacrifice through the fire of Your Divine Love!" [SS, pp. 204–5]

To offer herself in this way was for Thérèse no trifling vow, but the undertaking of a blood oath, to-the-death commitment. Discipleship meant ordering her life, to its last, most hidden second, to God. She was fully prepared for immolation by and for Christ, whatever form that might take.

She approached Pauline, who in 1893 had been elected prioress of Carmel, and hesitantly asked permission to offer herself in this new way. Pauline, accustomed to such seemingly overblown requests, replied that, assuming the notion was scripturally sound, she supposed the request could be granted. So Thérèse drafted a document, Pauline submitted it to a theologian, and two days later, Thérèse summoned Céline to the chapel where, kneeling side by side, Thérèse consecrated them both as "holocaust victims" to God's love. A few days later she tried to commandeer her sister Marie as well, asking: "Would *you* like to offer yourself as a victim to the merciful love of God?"—but as usual, the people closest to her didn't quite understand. Sister Marie replied, as I venture to say many of us would: "Indeed, no. God would take me at my word, and I have a great fear of suffering."

I, too, had a great fear of suffering. And while Marie eventually did similarly offer herself, and I could only pray to one day abandon myself more fully as well, this may be the place to reiterate that being a victim of love doesn't mean being a victim of situations that are of something other than love: the sickly, fear-based "martyrdom" that sometimes masquerades as love, for instance, or the misguided notion that our job is to do for others what they are capable of doing for themselves.

No, as Father Zossima observed in Dostoevsky's *The Brothers Karamasov*: "Love in reality is a harsh and dreadful thing compared to love in dreams." Thérèse knew all about this harsh love—and she would soon know even more. For on April 2, 1896, the eve of the Lenten celebration of Holy Thursday, and less than a year after having offered herself as a holocaust victim, she retired to her humble cell and suddenly coughed up a bubbling stream; "like a wave that was rising, rising, boiling up to my lips" [*SS*, p. 234].

Ever obedient, she complied with the rule that forbade lighting the lamp in her cell at night. When she checked the next morning, she found her handkerchief drenched in blood: the first sign of the tuberculosis that would eventually kill her. Her initial reaction was joy—she would go to Christ! She would enter heaven! She would offer herself up to be literally consumed (the disease of tuberculosis was colloquially known at the time as "consumption").

But what followed, as so often happens in the spiritual life, was not what Thérèse expected. What followed was not a blazing flame but the coldest, bleakest ashes. Almost immediately thereafter, she was plunged into frightful spiritual aridity, of an entirely different order, and almost infinitely worse, than anything that had come before.

She felt as if she were in a "dark tunnel," a "thick fog" [*SS*, p. 235]. The thought of heaven, which had previously presented itself with such certainty and sweetness, suddenly appeared to be a delusion:

It seems to me that the darkness, borrowing the voice of sinners, tells me mockingly, "You're dreaming up the light, this homeland smelling of sweetest perfume. You're dreaming up the *everlasting* possession of the Creator of all these marvelous things." [*SS*, p. 237]

She had always assumed that nonbelievers *chose* not to believe. Now, she learned otherwise:

During the most joyous days of Eastertide, Jesus made me feel that there truly are souls that don't have faith, who through the abuse of graces lose that precious treasure, the source of the only pure and true joy. He allowed my soul to be invaded by the thickest darkness, and for the thought of heaven, which was so sweet to me, to be only a subject of struggle and torment. . . . This trial was not to last for several days or weeks. It was to extend only to the time fixed by God, and . . . that time has not yet come. [*SS*, p. 235]

To the day she died, the darkness apparently never lifted. Thérèse's terrible dryness, coming at a time when she had to have known, however subliminally, that she was moving toward death, must have been a source of almost unbearable anguish. She pined to die a martyr—but how to die a martyr when there could scarcely have been "a soul that is *smaller* and more powerless than mine!" [*SS*, p. 216]. She had no advanced degrees. She'd crafted no elaborate metaphysical or theological theories.

So she searched, as she had so many times before, in Scripture. For years, in fact, Thérèse had read little else. She was steeped in the Psalms, the daily liturgy, the Gospels. Those with "eyes to see and ears to hear" (see Mark 8:18) find Scripture an inexhaustible fount of riches. For from a single verse, she ended up discovering the key to her whole "philosophy."

We know this, because in September 1896, a few months after Thérèse showed the first signs of TB, Sister Marie asked her to write a memoir of a retreat she had recently taken. The result, "Manuscript B," contains the heart of Thérèse's thought—the well-known treatise "My Vocation is Love"—and comprises chapter 9 in most versions of *The Story of a Soul*:

Here's her description of how the treatise came about:

> At prayer time my desires were making me suffer a true martyrdom, so I opened the letters of St. Paul in order to look for some sort of answer. Chapters 12 and 13 of the first letter to the Corinthians fell under my eyes. . . . I read the first of those chapters, that *everyone cannot* be apostles, prophets, teachers, etc.; that the Church is composed of different members, and that the eye cannot at *the same time* be a hand. . . .
>
> Considering the mystical body of the Church, I had not recognized myself in any of the members described by St. Paul, or rather, I wanted to recognize myself in *all of them*. . . . Charity gave me the key to my *vocation*. . . . I understood that Love alone can cause the members of

the Church to act. If Love were to be extinguished, the Apostles would no longer preach the gospel, the Martyrs would refuse to shed their blood. . . . I understood that *Love* contains all the Vocations, that Love is all, that it embraces all times and all places. . . . in a word, that it is Everlasting!

Then, in the excess of my delirious joy, I cried out, "Oh, Jesus, my Love. . . . I have finally found my vocation: My Vocation is Love!" [*SS*, pp. 216–17]

Marie was shocked by Thérèse's almost erotic passion, her desire for martyrdom. As always with Thérèse, however, the point was not her greatness, but God's; not the intensity of her desires, but rather the surrender of them: "My desires of martyrdom are nothing," she was quick to point out; "they are not what give me the unlimited confidence that I feel in my heart. . . . [Jesus] does not say that you must look for him among great souls, but from afar, that is to say in lowliness, in nothingness."

Lowliness, nothingness: "Oh, when I think how much I have to acquire," Céline once said to Thérèse; "*Rather, how much you have to lose,*" Thérèse replied.

Surrender—yet at the center of that surrender burned a white-hot flame. What does it mean to say that Thérèse let her flame burn hot? Fr. Ron Rolheiser points out that:

[F]rom the time of her "conversion," at age thirteen, when she overcame her hypersensitivity in her Christmas experience, leaving, as she put it, her childhood behind her, she began more and more to notice that what was true for her was less true for others. Their joys, pains, and dreams were not being noticed. Her mission then became that of "noticing the unnoticed drops of blood flowing out of the wounds of Christ." Thus, in the essential metaphor that undergirds her "little way" she writes:

"One Sunday, looking at a picture of Our Lord on the Cross, I was struck by the blood flowing from one of his divine hands. I felt a pang of great sorrow when thinking this blood was falling on the ground without anyone's hastening to gather it up. I was resolved to remain in spirit at the foot of the Cross and to receive its dew. Oh, I don't want this precious blood to be lost. I shall spend my life gathering it up for the good of souls. To live from love is to dry Your Face."

What Thérèse means by this metaphor is quite complex . . . but suffice it here to say the core of Thérèse's spirituality is not as much doing little hidden things for Christ as it is noticing the unnoticed drops of blood within the body of Christ, that is, noticing and valuing fully the unique and precious quality of other people's stories, tears, pains, and joys.

To let our own flames burn hot, then, requires a radical re-ordering of our time, energy, activities, attention, and orientation of heart. To let our flames burn hot requires asking: What is our stance toward "the least of these" (Matt.

25:31–46)? How much effort do we direct toward cultivating a prayer life? How hard do we try to wish our enemies well, to root out and let go of our resentments, to practice kindness, gentleness, humility? How do we spend our days? How many hours do we fritter away gossiping, complaining, delighting in others' misfortunes, mindlessly trolling the Internet, trying to win pointless political arguments?

Thérèse herself was seemingly oblivious to all political situations and most technological advancements. *The Story of a Soul* contains no mention of the Second Industrial Revolution, the world shortage of gold, the "long depression," as some historians call it, that spanned 1873–97: the exact years during which Thérèse lived. She saw the invention of the elevator not as a way to facilitate the erection of skyscrapers, but as a way to think about shortening the distance between us and Christ.

For that very reason, Thérèse's canonization near the beginning of a century that would see so many technological advancements and so much violence seems especially timely. Military force versus the vulnerability of humble charity. Nuclear power versus powerlessness. A public relations policy based neither on newspapers, nor on television, nor on cyberspace, nor on any mass movement, but on the movement of a single human heart.

"I have no other means of proving my love for You than to throw flowers, that is, not to pass up any little sacrifice, any look, any word, to take advantage of all the little things and to do them out of love" [*SS*, p. 220]. "There were no miracles, no raptures, no ecstasies—only service."

That after almost two thousand years, a pampered, bourgeois French girl could discover a fresh way to approach the Gospels only proves that even more riches are hidden in their pages. That an unschooled nun could become a Doctor of the Church only proves that more unexpected, astonishing, new ways of serving Christ await discovery. What had *I* discovered during my year with Thérèse? I'd started to ask. How had I evolved, if at all?

In the course of the year, I'd traveled to New Hampshire; New York City; Madison, Wisconsin; and California's central coast. I'd participated: with my friends, my family, my fellow alcoholics, my neighbors in Koreatown, the world at large. I'd worked hard and written as well as I could. I'd prayed, played the piano, watched the sun rise and set, studied the flowers and the birds, read widely, pondered deeply, shared meals, tended my plants, swooned to music, laughed, cried tears of joy and tears of pain. I'd lived life, in my way, to the hilt.

I had also pled, the whole year, to be wholly relieved of my romantic attachment; begged to stop loving so much. But I had finally been given to see that my desire was what made me human; that desire was my glory and my cross; that desire had given me a window onto the divine that would sustain me all my life. I had seen at least one person as God must see us—for where did my eyes come from but God?—and that is a rare and precious gift.

I could finally run into my friend and not feel devastated that he didn't "adore" me back. I could get a kick out of the common ground we did share. I could finally, genuinely want *other* people to love him, too. Maybe the wound would always hurt a little. I'd probably always be prone to getting snagged again. But those years of excruciating suffering had sharpened my desire so that the focus was basically "beyond." In fact the word *desire* comes from roots meaning "to the stars." Maybe that's what I'd learned from my time with Thérèse: My desire was on the stars.

In a 1940 letter Dorothy Day, that great devotee of Thérèse, writes of a story a friend had read:

> [I]n *The Saturday Evening Post* of all places . . . in which a young girl is wildly in love with a wastrel until later on when this had been broken up and she had been married for a year to a man of good solid character, she ran into her former love again. She confessed to her husband that she had been afraid of meeting him for fear some of the old glamour remained, and she said to him: "Now I can see him as he is." And her husband, who must have been a man of great discernment, said to her very sadly: "Perhaps it was before that you were seeing him as he really is." Or as he was meant to be, which is what he wanted to bring out.

All along, I had thought that the attachment, or midlife crisis, or dark night of the soul, or whatever my experience had been, was a terrible stumbling block, a sign of shameful weakness, evidence of some core, incurable insanity: in short, The Problem. Now I knew that, in some very difficult, mysterious way, it had actually been The Solution. My struggle went way beyond any relationship with, or way of seeing, a mere human being. All along, I had thought my error lay in failing to find the formula to love correctly, unselfishly, when the very idea of trying to perfect myself, with respect to human relationships—*or any other way*—was the real problem.

Forget trying to achieve your own holiness, Thérèse seemed to be saying: you are infinitely too feeble, weak, and misguided to accomplish anything on your own. You're like a bleating lamb, wandering blindly around with your divided, wayward heart. You're like a lost sheep, trying to get spiritual good marks by denying your humanity. You're like a straying member of the flock, off in a corner trying to heal your own wounds and relieve your own obsessions. Stop struggling, and the kingdom of God will be accomplished through you. Sit down on the floor, like a baby, and Christ will bend down and lift you up.

That is where you will get the strength to be a martyr. That is where you will get the courage to make your way through the suffering and loneliness of daily life. That is where you will get the joy to turn to the lost lamb beside you and assure him or her, as Christ assured the repentant thief as he hung on the cross: "Truly, I say to you, today you will be with me in Paradise" (Lk. 23:43).

As for my career, what is success but the ability to spend our days doing what we love? What is success but finding something or someone to whom we can give our whole mind, our whole strength, our whole heart, our whole will?

To dare to believe that we are truly loved, not for anything we have accomplished, earned, produced, learned, achieved, or sacrificed for, but simply for existing is a reality that can hardly be borne. We want that love more than anything; we search for that love all our lives. Yet we're somehow not able, not equipped to see it, perhaps, except by prolonged, sustained suffering—and uniting our suffering to Christ's. Thérèse did seem to be able to experience herself as fully loved—because she loved so much herself—and in the end that was perhaps her greatest gift: to God, to us.

We can't be afraid of looking foolish. We can't be afraid to let our desire burn hot no matter how much it hurts. We have to allow Christ to lift us up to him. We have to make our vocation love.

PRAYER

Lord, help me to be willing to live in the gap between the way things are and the way I wish they were.

Help me to be willing to hold the tension of a desire that can never be satisfied on this earth.

Help me not to try to anesthetize my pain by pretending I don't care, when the truth is that I do.

Help me to let the focus of my love go all the way to the stars, to Christ.

Help me to have the desires of a child, the fervor of a child, the trust of a child, the simplicity of a child.

Help me to remember that: "My sheep know my voice, and I know them, and they follow me."

THE DIVINE
ELEVATOR

(On Facing Death with Joy)

We're in an age of inventions. Now there's no more need to climb the steps of a staircase. In rich homes there are elevators that replace stairs to great advantage. I would also like to find an elevator to lift me up to Jesus, because I'm too little to climb the rough staircase of perfection. . . . The elevator that must lift me up to heaven is your arms, Jesus! For that I don't need to become big. On the contrary, I have to stay little—may I become little, more and more.

—*The Story of a Soul* [pp. 230–31]

I have no more desire to die than I have to live. From a natural point of view I would prefer death, but if I had a choice, I would not choose anything; I like only whatever God does.

—From the testimony of Agnes of Jesus
(Thérèse's sister Pauline)

[I]f in my childhood I suffered with sadness, I no longer suffer that way now: It's in joy and peace. I'm truly happy to suffer.

—*The Story of a Soul* [p. 233]

I was telling her that after her death, we would become very good and that the community would be renewed: "Amen, amen I say to you unless the grain of wheat falls into the ground and dies, it remains alone; but if it dies, it produces much fruit."

—Conversation between Agnes of Jesus (Thérèse's sister Pauline) and Thérèse, August 9, 1897

All through 1896 and the spring of 1897, Thérèse's condition steadily worsened. She underwent a treatment called *pointes de feu* (points of fire), during which her back was punctured hundreds of times with hot needles. She vomited and suffered from fevers. On May 18, 1897, overcome by nausea, chest pains, and coughing fits, she was relieved of all work.

Nonetheless, in June, 1897, Mother Marie de Gonzague, at Pauline's urging, directed Thérèse to pen what would be her last writings. Known as "Manuscript C," they comprise chapters 10 and 11 of *The Story of a Soul* and include the famous "Divine Elevator" passage quoted above.

Also nonetheless, we can never forget that for all her suffering, Thérèse experienced great, great joy: in Christ, in life, in her love of flowers, the seasons, snow. Even as she moved toward death, she was known in the cloister as one of the gayest, happiest nuns. She continued to sew, write letters, and work on her memoirs, as directed. She continued, as she had all her life, to be a spot-on mimic, nicknaming one of the doctors who attended her "Clodion the long-haired." She good-naturedly endured blistering poultices, the bad breath of the nuns who tended her, being heaped with blankets when she was already suffocating from heat.

She was always fasting, forever fasting, but as the Gospels tell us, when we fast, we don't wear a long face (Matt. 6:16–18). We don't make a show of fasting. We comb our hair, and we put on a clean shirt, and we go out into the world to support others in their own voluntary and involuntary fasts. We shore people up in a way that doesn't draw attention to itself so that people never know how much we are giving away and how deep the cost. We show up and we're cheerful and we have a joke, as Thérèse did even on July 6, 1897, the day she coughed up a lot of blood, "like liver." This period of spitting up blood (technical term: *haemoptysis*) would last until August 5th, during which time, though her condition was so serious that at one point the last rites were prepared, her usual light-heartedness continued: "It's really something to be in one's agony! But after all, what's that! I have sometimes been in agony over silly things."

Thérèse demonstrates two things we would do well to remember. First, she never made her life into some kind of warped, weird, private martyrdom. She may have been cloistered, but she was also fully engaged. During the last few years of her life, she corresponded with, and gave spiritual direction to, two missionaries—Maurice Bellière and Fr. Adolphe Roulland—whom she grew to love like brothers. She instructed her novices, was a sister among sisters, and prayed, sacrificed, and strove toward sanctity for all souls, everywhere, the whole time she was at Carmel.

Second, in loving others we have to continue to be open to our own terrible, terrible brokenness and wounds. We don't impose our vulnerabilities on people, but we have to be very in touch with them—with our weakness, our beggarliness—and we have to be able to share our entire selves with others without complaining or whining or making our frailties their problem. We have to thank people in a way for all they give us, even if what they often give is frustration and hurt. We don't commit emotional suicide. We rage against the dying of the light, and in the raging, we offer our death to others. In fact, Thérèse's greatest joy lay in her desire to continue working to save souls after her time on earth was through.

> During her last illness, at a time when she was in great pain, she said: "I am asking God that all the prayers that are said for me may be of benefit to sinners, and not for my relief." She wanted to go on working for souls even after her death; as she told Mother Agnes in my presence, she wanted to spend her heaven doing good on earth. Two months before she died, 22 July, 1897, I was reading her a passage on the happiness of heaven when she interrupted me: "That's not what attracts me." "What, then?" I asked. "Just love: to love, to be loved, and to come back on earth to make Love loved."

By the end, Thérèse had intestinal gangrene and only a quarter of one lung left. To the end, she continued to display the patience, good cheer, and self-control that were her hallmarks. During the last several months of her life, when her sanctity had at last come to be suspected, Pauline kept the "Yellow Notebook" in which were recorded what have come to be known, along with other assorted remarks, remembrances, and letters, as *Her Last Conversations*.

Samples:

Would you be happy if you were told you would die in a few days at the latest? You would prefer this to being told that you will suffer more and more for months and years?

"Oh! no, I wouldn't be at all happier. What makes me happy is only to do the will of God."

If you were to die tomorrow, wouldn't you be afraid? It would be so close!

"Ah! even this evening, I wouldn't be afraid; I would only be filled with joy."

These days Pauline would have been running a videocam. As it was, she seemed to have madly recorded every last sigh, tear, quip, and desire—"During the afternoon silence, I was hiding in back of the bed in order to write something down"; "She spoke to me a long time about this subject, and I was not able to write it all down"—meanwhile pestering Thérèse, however unintentionally, with the most annoying, obnoxious questions imaginable:

You prefer to die rather than live?

If someone told you that you would die suddenly, at this instant, would you be afraid?

Then you prefer dying to living?

Well, now you are content? [after the doctor left].

If you were made to choose one or the other [to die in agony or not to die in agony], which would you choose?"

Does what you will become disturb you?

Time must seem long to you. What a terrible sickness and how much you're suffering.

Would you drink this cup [of milk] to save my life?

Someone found you imperfect on a certain occasion.

Are you discouraged?

You don't have any intuition about the day of your death?

Thérèse *must* have been a saint not to have snapped, *I'm not a fortuneteller, for heaven's sake. Now go fetch me some pain pills.*

Instead, she suffered not only the morbid, intrusive questions of her fellow nuns, but what must have been far worse: the continuing doubts about her faith. Reading of Thérèse's last days, again and again I turned to the photo at the front of Ida Görres's *The Hidden Face*. This was no airbrushed, prettified likeness—for we tend to like our saints prettified—but a face annealed by such intense suffering that Thérèse looked almost angry, the face of a person whose body has slowly burned itself out from within and is down to its last cauterizing ember.

I was reminded of Catholic novelist Flannery O'Connor's definition of a freak: an "answer to a riddle that was more puzzling than the riddle itself." What mysterious and dreadful love had called this young girl to give herself body, soul, and spirit, to God? Love transforms, but love first consumes. "I am not dying; I am entering life," she had written to one of her spiritual brothers, Fr. Bellière, but anyone who has witnessed a death knows that dying is a terrible travail, a labor to bring about a different kind of birth. We are called to hold the unbearable tension between two kinds of fire: the fire of our self-will and the fire of God's purifying love. To bring good where there is evil, light where there is darkness, and solace to a world in peril is a fearsome undertaking.

And yet we are doing it. We are doing it every time we hold our tongue when the sharp retort rushes to our lips; every time we silently let someone off the hook; with every thank-you note, every prayer, every yes, every breath. To pick up a pin for love can convert a soul. Not for virtue, not for merit, but for love. Not so that we can be saved, but so that the next person can. Not to relieve our suffering, but to make up for what is lacking in the suffering of Christ.

On July 30th, suffocating, Thérèse was anointed. From August 19th on, she could no longer receive the Eucharist, lest she vomit. Grasping her crucifix in the following weeks, kissing Jesus' face, she gasped of the pain, "It's enough to make one go out of one's mind." Dr. de Cornière, the attending physician, suggested morphine, but Mother de Gonzague would not allow it.

On Wednesday, September 29, Thérèse gave her last confession. On September 30, toward 5 PM, she told Pauline: "Never would I have believed it was possible to suffer so much! never! never! I cannot explain this except by the ardent desires I have had to save souls."

The other nuns were called to her room. According to Pauline:

> For more than two hours a terrible rattle tore her chest. Her face was blue, her hands purplish, her feet were cold, and she shook in all her members. Perspiration stood out in enormous drops on her forehead and rolled down her cheeks. Her difficulties in breathing were always increasing, and in order to breathe she made involuntary little cries. All during this time, so full of agony for us, we heard through the window . . . the twittering of robins.

The nuns prayed, kept watch, wrung their hands. Mother de Gonzague finally sent them away.

Twenty minutes later, Thérèse raised her head and said, "Mother! Isn't this the agony?"

The nuns were summoned again.

Gazing at the crucifix, Thérèse breathed her last, crying: "Oh! I love him! My God, I love You!"

Seldom have we felt so keenly the loneliness of the saint; of Christ in the Garden of Gethsemane; of the rest of us who trudge the spiritual path in obscurity, fatigue, and pain. We want people to be kind to us, and we're called to be kind to them. We want to be cared for, and we're called to sacrifice. We want prosperity, but real life looks more like Good Friday.

I think of my friend Fred, who died near the end of my year with Thérèse. Fred had three roommates in his ward at the VA Hospital, one, Mr. Large, to whom Fred—irascible, curmudgeonly, Fred—had taken a special liking. Mr. Large responded to Fred's ministrations, if at all, with a noncommittal grunt, but Fred was tireless. He'd jump up to whisk away straws and stray bits of plastic—Jell-O lids, syringe wrappings—from beneath Mr. Large's bed. He'd snatch up his favorite Cardinals cap and lovingly plant it on Mr. Large's balding skull. He'd help Mr. Large with his socks, kneeling at his feet the way Jesus knelt to wash the feet of the disciples the night before he died.

We seem not to attain our full significance until we do die: Thérèse recognized at last as a saint by the nuns with whom she had lived; canonized within twenty-eight years of her death; a century later beloved the world over, with miracles attributed to her name, basilicas dedicated to her memory, and her "little way" enshrined in a million hearts.

Fred could be difficult. We tangled many times. But now that he's gone, I don't remember any of the hardness. I remember how good he was, how much he suffered. I remember him helping Mr. Large with his socks.

PRAYER

Thérèse, by your generous intercession:

May we, too, suffer in joy and peace.

May we, too, like only whatever God does.

May we, too, see that we are often in agony over silly things.

May we, too, be patient with those who annoy us when we're in pain.

May we, too, praise the trees, the birds, the flowers.

May we, too, know that unless the grain of wheat falls into the ground and dies, it remains alone; but if it dies, it produces much fruit.

May we, too, become little—more and more.

— APPENDIX A —

THE MARTIN FAMILY, IN BRIEF

FATHER: Louis Martin, jeweler
MOTHER: Zélie Martin, lacemaker.

THEIR FIVE DAUGHTERS (four other children had died at
  birth or in infancy), all of whom became nuns:

MARIE (OF THE SACRED HEART): b. 2-22-1860,
  entered Carmel 10-15-1886.

PAULINE (AGNES OF JESUS): b. 9-7-1861,
  entered Carmel 10-2-1882. (Mother Agnes of Jesus and
  Mother Marie of the Sacred Heart alternated as prioress of the
  Carmel for many years).

LÉONIE (FRANÇOISE THÉRÈSE): b. 6-3-1863,
  first entered Poor Clares October 7, 1886, entered Visitation
  Convent (permanently) 1-29-1899.

CÉLINE (SISTER GENEVIÈVE): b. 4-28-1869,
  entered Carmel 9-14-1894.

THÉRÈSE (OF THE HOLY FACE): b. 1-2-1873,
  entered Carmel 4-9-1888, d. 9-30-1897.

CHRONOLOGY OF THÉRÈSE'S LIFE

JANUARY 2, 1873: Thérèse is born.

JANUARY 4, 1873: Thérèse is baptized, when she is three days old.

AUGUST 28, 1877: Thérèse's mother, Zélie, dies when Thérèse is four and a half years old.

1883: at eight and a half, Thérèse begins attending day school run by Benedictine nuns at Lisieux.

MARCH 25, 1883: When she is ten and a half, Thérèse undergoes a mysterious illness, possibly neurological, that resembled a kind of possession; she is cured May 13, 1883, by the smile of a statue of the Blessed Virgin Mary.

MAY 8, 1884: At the age of eleven, Thérèse makes her First Communion.

MAY 1885–NOVEMBER 1886: At the age of thirteen, Thérèse suffers a case of "scruples" (neurotic hyper-guilt) so severe that, coupled with Marie leaving home on October 15, 1886, to enter the convent, Thérèse withdraws from the Benedictine day school and resumes being educated at home.

CHRISTMAS EVE, 1886: Thérèse experiences her "second conversion."

SEPTEMBER 1, 1887: The criminal Pranzini, for whom Thérèse has prayed, is executed.

NOVEMBER 20, 1887: At the age of fourteen, Thérèse has an audience with Pope Leo XIII at which she kneels at the Pope's feet and pleads: "Most Holy Father, I have a great grace to ask of you! . . . Most Holy Father, in honor of your jubilee, allow me to enter Carmel at the age of fifteen."

APRIL 9, 1888: At the age of fifteen, Thérèse enters Carmel.

JUNE 1988: Louis Martin shows the first signs of dementia.

JANUARY 9, 1889: Thérèse's reception of the habit ("the clothing").

JANUARY 10, 1889–SEPTEMBER 24, 1890: Thérèse's novitiate.

SEPTEMBER 8, 1890: Thérèse makes her Profession, binding herself forever to the vows of poverty, chastity, and obedience.

SEPTEMBER 24, 1890: Thérèse takes the veil.

DECEMBER 1890: Influenza breaks out in Carmel.

MAY 1892: Thérèse sees her father for the last time, in the parlor at Carmel.

JULY 29, 1894: Thérèse's father, Louis Martin, dies.

WINTER 1894: Mother Pauline, at Mother Marie of the Sacred Heart's urging, orders Thérèse, twenty-one at the time, to write the memoirs of her childhood. (The result, "Manuscript A," comprises chapters 1 through 8 of her autobiography, *The Story of a Soul*.)

JUNE 9, 1895: Thérèse offers herself as a "holocaust victim" of Love.

APRIL 2–3, 1896: On the eve of the Lenten celebration of Holy Thursday, Thérèse, then twenty-three, coughs up liquid and in the morning, finds her handkerchief drenched in blood: the first symptom of tuberculosis. Feeling great joy at first, she is quickly plunged into frightful spiritual aridity.

SEPTEMBER 1896: Sister Marie asks Thérèse to write a memoir of a retreat she had recently taken. (The result, "Manuscript B," comprises chapter 9 of *The Story of a Soul* and contains the well-known treatise, dated September 1896: "My Vocation is Love.")

JUNE 1897: Three months before Thérèse's death: Mother Marie de Gonzague, the superior of Carmel, directs Thérèse to write what will become "Manuscript C," comprising chapters 10 and 11 of *The Story of a Soul* and containing, among other things, the "Divine Elevator" passage and an explanation of Thérèse's "little way."

SEPTEMBER 30, 1897: Thérèse dies at the age of twenty-four.

JUNE 9, 1914: Thérèse's Cause of Beatification is introduced in Rome.

MAY 17, 1925: Thérèse is declared a saint.

JANUARY 18, 1940: Marie dies.

JUNE 17, 1941: Léonie dies.

JUNE 28, 1951: Pauline dies.

FEBRUARY 25, 1959: Céline, the last of the Martin family, dies in the Carmel of Lisieux.

OCTOBER 19, 1997: Thérèse is declared a Doctor of the Church by Rome.

NOTES AND PERMISSIONS

xiii *At each new opportunity to do battle* Excerpts from
The Story of a Soul quoted in this book are taken from
Robert J. Edmonson, cj, trans., *The Story of a Soul: A New
Translation* (Brewster, MA: Paraclete Press, 2006). These
excerpts are indicated by "*The Story of a Soul*" or simply
"*SS*," followed by the page number from which they were
taken, and are used by permission of Paraclete Press,
Inc.

xiv *I imagine myself at Nazareth* Ida Friederike Görres,
The Hidden Face: A Study of St. Thérèse of Lisieux, trans.
from German by Richard and Clara Winston (New York:
Pantheon, 1959), 303–4, quoting Thérèse; see also *The
Complete Thérèse of Lisieux,* translated and edited by
Robert J. Edmonson, cj (Brewster, MA: Paraclete Press,
2009), 287.

xvii *I'm of a nature such that fear causes me to draw back* Guy
Gaucher, *The Spiritual Journey of St. Thérèse of Lisieux*
(London: Dartman, Longman, and Todd, 1987), 109.

xvii *There can be no doubt that as a matter of fact a religious
life* William James, *The Varieties of Religious Experience*
(New York: New American Library, 1958), 24.

9   *Thérèse of Lisieux fascinates us*   Ronald Rolheiser, http://www.ronrolheiser.com/common/pdf/perennial. pdf, p. 1, accessed November 21, 2010. Excerpts from this document are used by permission of Ronald Rolheiser.

9   *Inside of each of us*   Rolheiser, 6.

10   *Who could ever invent the Blessed Virgin?*   Conversation from August 31, 1897, in *St. Therese of Lisieux: Her Last Conversations*, John Clarke, OCD, trans. Copyright © 1977 Washington Province of Discalced Carmelites. ICS Publications, 2131 Lincoln Road, N.E., Washington DC 2002-1199, U.S.A. www.icspublications.org. This excerpt is from p. 176. All excerpts from this book are used by permission.

13   *It is impossible to write a book*   Caryll Houselander, *Guilt* (London: London, Sheed & Ward, 1952), 230.

18   *[S]he could abandon her wild despair*   Görres, *The Hidden Face,* 79.

25   *Thérèse could pour out bucketfuls of reverential tears*   Görres, *The Hidden Face*, 97.

30   *[The woman] will need great courage*   Helen M. Luke, *Kaleidoscope: The Way of Woman and Other Essays* (New York: Parabola Books, 1992), 41.

32 *[T]o give up a misery*   Luke, 150.

37 *Clearly the distance was not a problem for her*   Lorenzo Albacete, *God at the Ritz* (New York: Crossroad Publishing, 2002), 155–56.

41 *You know well you are taking care of a little saint* Conversation from August, 1897, in Clarke, *Her Last Conversations*, 263.

44 *Disobedience to authority, at the right moment*   Luke, 96.

47 *Stay in me as you do in the tabernacle*   Testimony of Agnes of Jesus (Thérèse's sister Pauline) in *St. Thérèse of Lisieux: By Those Who Knew Her,* Testimonies from the process of beatification, ed. and trans. by Christopher O'Mahony, OCD (San Francisco: Ignatius Press, 1989), 48. The excerpts from this book are used by permission of Ignatius Press.

49 *[S]he toyed with the idea of joining*   Testimony of Geneviève of Saint Teresa (Thérèse's sister Céline) in O'Mahony, 116–17.

50 *For Thérèse, chastity meant two, interpenetrating, things*   Rolheiser, 11.

57 *I found the community in a very disappointing state*   From the testimony of Mary Magdalene of the Blessed Sacrament in O'Mahony, 260.

60 *Tall and strong, with the air of a child*   *Derniers Entretiens*, 1: 137, n. 149, Mother de Gonzague to the Visitation Convent; taken from Clarke, *Her Last Conversations*, 16.

62 *When you are exasperated with someone*   Thérèse's sister Céline, quoting Thérèse, in O'Mahony, 132.

69 *Her "little way" consisted in boasting*   From the testimony of Geneviève of Saint Teresa (Thérèse's sister Céline) in O'Mahony, 136.

71 *[The "little way"] was a matter of allowing*   Joseph F. Schmidt, FSC, *Everything is Grace: The Life and Way of Thérèse of Lisieux* (Ijamsville, MD: The Word Among Us, 2007), 224.

71 *How often I have thought that perhaps*   Conversation from July 15, 1897, in Clarke, *Her Last Conversations*, 99–100.

72 *When I can feel nothing, when I am altogether arid*   Görres, *The Hidden Face*, 343.

74 *The city is the place of human pride*   *The Jerusalem Community, Rule of Life*, Sr. Kathleen England, tr. (London, UK: Darton Longman and Todd, Ltd., 1985), 129. Quoted in *Magnificat*, Meditation of the Day, July 13, 2003.

75 *It comes as no great surprise to discover*   Robert A. Johnson, *Owning Your Own Shadow* (San Francisco: HarperSanFrancisco, 1991), 61–62.

76 *The whole way along the human religious itinerary*   Luigi Giussani, *At the Origin of the Christian Claim* (Québec: McGill-Queen's University Press, 1998), 4.

76 *[S]he rejected all ascetic efforts*   Görres, *The Hidden Face*, 331.

77 *There is nothing outwardly to distinguish a Saint*   Coventry Patmore, *The Rod, the Root, and the Flower* (London: George Bell and Sons, 1907), 160–62.

81 *She had perhaps expected to find in Carmel*   Étienne Robo, *Two Portraits of St. Thérèse of Lisieux* (Chicago: Henry Regnery Company, 1955), 77.

82 *She believed it was wrong to be afraid*   From the testimony of Geneviève of Saint Teresa (Thérèse's sister Céline), in O'Mahony, 125.

87 *The ritual event*   Carl Jung, "Transformation Symbolism in the Mass," in *Psyche and Symbol*, trans. R.F.C Hull (Princeton, NJ: Princeton University Press 1991), 204, 206.

93 *If you are willing to bear serenely*   Görres, *The Hidden Face*, 330, quoting Thérèse.

95 *It would certainly be unfair*   Ida Friederike Görres, *Broken Lights: Diaries & Letters (1951–59)* (London: Burns & Oates, 1964). Quoted in http://en.wikipedia.org/wiki/Th%C3%A9r%C3%A8se_of_Lisieux, accessed April 12, 2011.

100 *You alone have sought my soul!*   English translation by Margaret Chanler in *Hymns to the Church* (New York: Sheed and Ward, 1953), 20, slightly amended by Erasmo Leiva-Merakakis. Reprinted by permission of Sheed and Ward, an imprint of Rowman & Littlefield Publishers, Inc., and by Erasmo Leiva-Kerikakis, now Br. Simeon Leiva, ocso, of St. Joseph's Abbey, Spencer, MA.

105 *Of her life in the convent there is little*   Robo, 25.

105 *There was nothing to say about her*   Guy Gaucher, *The Story of a Life: St. Thérèse of Lisieux* (New York: Harper Collins, 1993), 207.

105 *She considered it harder for human nature*   From the testimony of Geneviève of Saint Teresa (Thérèse's sister Céline) in O'Mahony, 116–17.

107 *I said to myself: And this blessed child* Clarke, *Her Last Conversations*, 18.

113 *Failure, then failure! so the world stamps us* William James, *The Varieties of Religious Experience* (New York: New American Library, 1958), 119–20.

115 *In the seven years since she'd entered Carmel* Görres, *The Hidden Face*, 271.

115 *The great saints have worked for God's glory* Clarke, *Her Last Conversations*, 239.

117 *Would you like to offer yourself* Gaucher, *The Story of a Life*, 148.

121 *My desires of martyrdom are nothing* From Letter 197, from Thérèse to Marie, dated Sept. 17th, 1896, *The Letters of St. Thérèse of Lisieux and Those Who Knew Her: General Correspondence,* vol. 2, ed. by John Clarke, OCD (Washington, D.C.: ICS Publications, 1982).

121 *Oh, when I think how much* Sister Geneviève of the Holy Face (Céline Martin), *My Sister Saint Thérèse* (Rockford, IL: Tan Books and Publishers, Inc., 1997), 28.

121 *[F]rom the time of her "conversion"* Rolheiser, 11. The footnotes in this excerpt have been omitted.

123 *There were no miracles*   Clarke, *Her Last Conversations*, 235.

125 *[I]n* The Saturday Evening Post   Dorothy Day, from a letter to the *Buffalo Catholic Worker*, undated, 1940, in *All the Way to Heaven: The Selected Letters of Dorothy Day*, ed. Robert Ellsberg (Milwaukee, WI: Marquette University Press, 2010), 122.

129 *I have no more desire to die*   From the testimony of Agnes of Jesus (Thérèse's sister Pauline), in O'Mahony, 67.

130 *I was telling her that after her death*   Conversation between Agnes of Jesus (Thérèse's sister Pauline) and Thérèse, August 9, 1897, in Clarke, *Her Last Conversations*, 145.

131 *It's really something to be in one's agony*   July 8, 1897, in Clarke, *Her Last Conversations*, 80.

132 *During her last illness*   From the testimony of Geneviève of Saint Teresa (Thérèse's sister Céline), in O'Mahony, 131.

133 *Oh! no, I wouldn't be at all*   August 30, 1897, in Clarke, *Her Last Conversations*, 175.

133 *Ah! even this evening, I wouldn't* August 31, 1897, in Clarke, *Her Last Conversations,* 176.

133 *During the afternoon silence* August 18, 1897, in Clarke, *Her Last Conversations,* 152.

133 *She spoke to me a long time* August 20, 1897, in Clarke, *Her Last Conversations,* 159.

134 *You prefer to die rather than live?* September 4, 1897, in Clarke, *Her Last Conversations,* 183.

134 *If someone told you that you* September 10, 1897, in Clarke, *Her Last Conversations,* 187.

134 *Then you prefer dying to living?* September 5, 1897, in Clarke, *Her Last Conversations,* 184.

134 *Well, now you are content?* September 10, 1897, in Clarke, *Her Last Conversations,* 187.

134 *If you were made to choose* September 14, 1897, in Clarke, *Her Last Conversations,* 190.

134   *Does what you will become*   August 15, 1897, in Clarke,
      Her Last Conversations, 149.

134   *Time must seem long to you*   September 22, 1897, in
      Clarke, *Her Last Conversations,* 196.

134   *Would you drink this cup*   August 20, 1897, in Clarke,
      Her Last Conversations, 156.

134   *Someone found you imperfect*   August 22, 1897, in
      Clarke, *Her Last Conversations,* 162.

134   *Are you discouraged?*   August 24, 1897, in Clarke, *Her
      Last Conversations,* 166.

134   *You don't have any intuition*   September 24, 1897, in
      Clarke, *Her Last Conversations,* 199.

135   *I am not dying*   Clarke, *The Letters of St. Thérèse of Lisieux
      and Those Who Knew Her,* 244.

136   *It's enough to make one go*   August 22, 1897, in Clarke,
      Her Last Conversations, 162, fn.

136   *Never would I have believed*   September 30, 1897, in
      Clarke, *Her Last Conversations,* 205.

136   *For more than two hours*   September 30, 1897, in Clarke, *Her Last Conversations,* 206.

SELECTED BIBLIOGRAPHY

Albacete, Lorenzo. *God at the Ritz*. New York: Crossroad Publishing, 2002.

Clarke, John, OCD, ed. *The Letters of St. Thérèse of Lisieux and Those Who Knew Her: General Correspondence, Volume 2*. Washington, D.C.: ICS Publications, 1982.

————, trans. from the original manuscript. *St. Therese of Liseux: Her Last Conversations*. Washington, D.C.: ICS Publications, 1977.

Day, Dorothy. *Thérèse: A Life of Thérèse of Lisieux*. Springfield, IL: Templegate Publishers, 1960.

De Meester, Conrad, ed. *Saint Thérèse of Lisieux: Her Life, Times, and Teaching*. Washington, D.C.: ICS Publications, 1997.

Edmonson, Robert J., CJ, trans. and ed. *The Complete Thérèse of Lisieux*. Brewster, MA: Paraclete Press, 2009.

————, trans. and ed. *The Story of a Soul, A New Translation: St. Thérèse of Lisieux*. Brewster, MA: Paraclete Press, 2006.

Ellsberg, Robert, ed. *All the Way to Heaven: The Selected Letters of Dorothy Day*. Milwaukee, WI: Marquette University Press, 2010.

Gaucher, Guy. *The Spiritual Journey of St. Thérèse of Lisieux*. London: Dartman, Longman, and Todd, 1987.

———. *The Story of a Life: St. Thérèse of Lisieux*. New York: Harper Collins, 1993.

Giussani, Luigi. *At the Origin of the Christian Claim*. Québec: McGill-Queen's University Press, 1998.

Görres, Ida Friederike. *Broken Lights: Diaries & Letters (1951–59)*. London: Burns & Oates, 1964.

———. *The Hidden Face: A Study of St. Thérèse of Lisieux*. Richard and Clara Winston, trans. from German. New York: Pantheon, 1959.

Houselander, Caryll. *Guilt*. London: London, Sheed & Ward, 1952.

James, William. *The Varieties of Religious Experience*. New York: New American Library, 1958.

Johnson, Robert A. *Owning Your Own Shadow*. San Francisco, CA: HarperSanFrancisco, 1991.

Jung, Carl. "Transformation Symbolism in the Mass," essay in *Psyche and Symbol*. R.F.C. Hull, trans. Princeton, NJ: Princeton University Press 1991.

Laird, Martin. *Into the Silent Land: A Guide to the Christian Practice of Contemplation*. New York: Oxford University Press, 2005.

Luke, Helen M. *Kaleidoscope: The Way of Woman and Other Essays*. New York: Parabola Books, 1992.

May, Gerald G., M.D. *The Awakened Heart*. New York: Harper Collins, 1991.

O'Connor, Patricia. *Thérèse of Lisieux: A Biography*. Huntington, IN: Our Sunday Visitor, 1983.

O'Mahony, Christopher, OCD, ed. and trans. *St. Thérèse of Lisieux: By Those Who Knew Her*. Testimonies from the process of beatification. San Francisco: Ignatius Press, 1989.

Patmore, Coventry. *The Rod, the Root, and the Flower*. London: George Bell and Sons, 1907.

Payne, Steven, OCD. *Saint Thérèse of Lisieux: Doctor of the Universal Church*. New York: Alba House, 2002.

Robo, Étienne. *Two Portraits of St. Thérèse of Lisieux*. Chicago: Henry Regnery Company, 1955.

Schmidt, Joseph F., FSC. *Everything is Grace: The Life and Way of Thérèse of Lisieux*. Ijamsville, MD: The Word Among Us, 2007.

St. Thérèse of Lisieux: Essential Writings. Selected with an introduction by Mary Frolich. New York: Orbis Books, 2003.

von le Fort, Gertrud. *Hymns to the Church*. Margaret Chanler, trans. New York: Sheed and Ward, 1953.

ABOUT PARACLETE PRESS

WHO WE ARE

Paraclete Press is a publisher of books, recordings, and DVDs on Christian spirituality. Our publishing represents a full expression of Christian belief and practice—from Catholic to Evangelical, from Protestant to Orthodox.

We are the publishing arm of the Community of Jesus, an ecumenical monastic community in the Benedictine tradition. As such, we are uniquely positioned in the marketplace without connection to a large corporation and with informal relationships to many branches and denominations of faith.

WHAT WE ARE DOING

Books

Paraclete publishes books that show the richness and depth of what it means to be Christian. Although Benedictine spirituality is at the heart of all that we do, we publish books that reflect the Christian experience across many cultures, time periods, and houses of worship. We publish books that nourish the vibrant life of the church and its people—books about spiritual practice, formation, history, ideas, and customs.

We have several different series, including the best-selling Paraclete Essentials, and Paraclete Giants series of classic texts in contemporary English; A Voice from the Monastery—men and women monastics writing about living a spiritual life today; award-winning literary faith fiction and poetry; and the Active Prayer Series that brings creativity and liveliness to any life of prayer.

Recordings

From Gregorian chant to contemporary American choral works, our music recordings celebrate sacred choral music through the centuries. Paraclete distributes the recordings of the internationally acclaimed choir Gloriæ Dei Cantores, praised for their "rapt and fathomless spiritual intensity" by *American Record Guide,* and the Gloriæ Dei Cantores Schola, which specializes in the study and performance of Gregorian chant. Paraclete is also the exclusive North American distributor of the recordings of the Monastic Choir of St. Peter's Abbey in Solesmes, France, long considered to be a leading authority on Gregorian chant.

DVDs

Our DVDs offer spiritual help, healing, and biblical guidance for life issues: grief and loss, marriage, forgiveness, anger management, facing death, and spiritual formation.

Learn more about us at our website:
www.paracletepress.com,
or call us toll-free at 1-800-451-5006.

A Little Daily Wisdom
*Through the Year with
Saint Teresa of Avila*

By Bernard Bangley

ISBN: 978-155725-697-3
$16.99, Trade paper

St. Teresa of Avila is not a lofty, inaccessible saint; she's a companion, and has been taking Christians on a journey through their own interior "castles" for hundreds of years. Honest, humorous, and insightful, her devotional and spiritual reflections show you how to open up yourself to God in new ways.

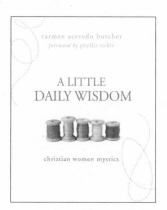

A Little Daily Wisdom
Christian Women Mystics

By Carmen Acevedo Butcher

ISBN: 978-155725-586-0
$14.95, Trade paper

Discover the strength, wisdom, and joyful faith of Christianity's legendary women—the medieval mystics. Their honesty and deep love for God will encourage and empower you every day of the year.

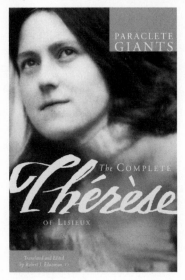

The Complete Thérèse of Lisieux
Translated and Edited by Robert J. Edmonson, CJ

ISBN: 978-155725-670-6 $24.99, Paperback

*A complete and engaging one-volume introduction
to the saint known as the "Little Flower"*

INCLUDES:
- the classic *The Story of a Soul,* complete and unabridged
- rarely seen, her sisters' description of her final days
- a poignant collection of anecdotes about Thérèse recounted after her death
- prayers, letters, and poems, including the poem that inspired the name "Little Flower"
- appendices, engravings, and rare photographs

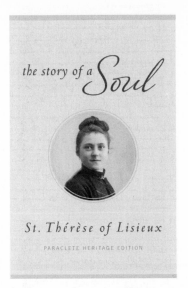

The Story of a Soul—St. Thérèse of Lisieux

PARACLETE HERITAGE EDITION

ISBN: 978-155725-693-5 $24.00, Hardcover

*A beautifully modernized translation of the most beloved
Catholic classic of the twentieth century*

Millions of hearts have been touched by St. Thérèse's desire to be a
humble, "little flower" that would be a delight to God's "eyes."

Written in obedience to her Carmelite superior, Thérèse's personal
story was edited and published following her death in 1897 at
the age of twenty-four. Combining charming descriptions of her
family with accounts of her foibles, her sense of humor, radical
honesty, and intense devotion to God made this autobiography an
instant bestseller.

The St. Thérèse of Lisieux
Prayer Book

Vinita Hampton Wright

ISBN: 978-155725-578-5 $15.99, French Flap

The wisdom of St. Thérèse of Lisieux—for all who want to pray

Millions of people know and love St. Thérèse—the world's most popular saint during the first half of the twentieth century.

This warm, wise little book will help you to discover firsthand how to receive God's presence and love. You will:

- Walk with Thérèse through days of humility, suffering, beauty, and spiritual sensitivity.
- Discover through prayer and growing faith, how you too can follow your own Little Way to authentic Christian experience.

Available from most booksellers or through Paraclete Press:
www.paracletepress.com; 1-800-451-5006.
Try your local bookstore first.